The American Revolution and the Declaration of Independence

The American Revolution and the Declaration of Independence

THE ESSAYS OF
GEORGE H. SMITH

CATO INSTITUTE
WASHINGTON, D.C.

eBook ISBN: 978-1-944424-49-7
Print ISBN: 978-1-944424-48-0

Library of Congress Cataloging-in-Publication Data available.

Cover design: Faceout.
Printed in the United States of America.

CATO INSTITUTE
1000 Massachusetts Avenue, N.W.
Washington, D.C. 20001
www.cato.org

CONTENTS

Independence Day: What Is There to Celebrate?

The Fourth of July is upon us once again—time for many Americans to fly the flag, take the tots to see local fireworks, and praise America as the greatest country that has existed in the annals of humankind or that ever will exist until the sun burns out.

I enjoy holidays as much as anyone else does. They give me a respectable excuse to avoid working and to do so with a clear conscience, even if I am late on a deadline. I applaud any plausible rationale for guilt-free indolence, and I harbor a deep resentment against the Protestant Reformers, especially the puritans, for abolishing many of the traditional Catholic holidays.

In the tradition of Aristotle, as channeled through Aquinas and other medieval philosophers, Catholic intellectuals tended to view work as a means to the end of leisure, and leisure as the time when we do things for their own sake rather than for the sake of something else. Then along came some grim Protestants who promoted a view that was later called the Protestant work ethic, according to which work is an end in itself and leisure is to be feared as the devil's playground.

H. L. Mencken had a point when he defined *puritanism* as "the haunting fear that someone, somewhere, may be happy." So did the great English historian T. B. Macaulay when he wrote, "The puritan hated bear baiting, not because it gave pain to the bear, but because it gave pleasure to the spectators." Then there is the joke about a puritan minister who, when asked if it is sinful for a married couple to experience simultaneous orgasms during sex, replied, "Two wrongs don't make a right."

Nevertheless, even the most puritanical among us have enthusiastically embraced Independence Day as a time for pleasure. Cantankerous John Adams, a puritan in spirit if not in doctrine, believed that Independence Day "ought to be solemnized with Pomp and Parade, with Shews, Games, Sports, Guns, Bells, Bonfires and Illuminations from one End of this Continent to the other from this Time forward forever more."

John's hopeful prediction did not quite pan out. It is well known, for example, that he expected Independence Day to be celebrated on the second of July, since that was when American independence was officially proclaimed by the Second Continental Congress. In addition, John did not anticipate that some of the festivities he recommended would later become illegal. Celebrate the Fourth of July with a gun and you might land in jail. If you want a bonfire or parade, you will need a special government permit. And depending on your state, the private use of fireworks ("illuminations") might get you arrested. Ironically, consumer fireworks are banned in Massachusetts, John's beloved home state, so if he were alive today and wanted to follow his own advice, he would need to go elsewhere to celebrate freedom *legally*.

Exactly *what* are we celebrating on the Fourth of July? More specifically, is there anything about Independence Day that *libertarians* should celebrate?

Well, there was the formal separation of 13 American colonies from the British Empire, but that doesn't explain the exuberance of our contemporary celebrations. And there is the bit about "No taxation without representation"—a slogan that has little meaning today and, contrary to popular opinion, was rarely if ever heard during protests against British measures. Moreover, "No taxation without representation" is misleading because it suggests that colonials would have agreed to be taxed if they could elect their own representatives to serve in the British Parliament, whereas virtually all radicals expressly repudiated that option. Nor is it true that the colonials would have passively paid taxes that were authorized by their own legislatures. Quite the contrary; as the historian Robert Palmer wryly observed in his two-volume masterpiece, *The Age of the Democratic Revolution*, "One suspects that 'no taxation without representation' meant no taxation with representation, either."[1]

According to Palmer, "The British Americans enjoyed a lighter tax burden than [almost] any other people of the Western World." Americans "paid no direct taxes, and not much in the way of customs duties, to the central government." British Americans enjoyed many other freedoms as well, and this fact led some skeptics, including some modern historians, to question the motives of those Americans who fought against the British during the Revolution. Why would a people with so much freedom—more freedom than found anywhere in Europe and more freedom, in certain crucial areas, than Americans enjoy today—take up arms against a relatively benign government?

Thomas Paine addressed this issue in *Letter to the Abbé Raynal* (1782). Calling the Stamp Act (1765) "a slight tax upon the colonies," Raynal could not understand why it provoked ferocious resistance in America. After all, colonial America was not ruled by an arbitrary power. "Morals there had not been insulted. Manners, customs, habits, no object dear to nations, had there been the sport of ridicule."

Paine replied that it was not the amount of the stamp tax, large or small, that inspired widespread, violent resistance. Rather, Americans viewed the new tax as a dangerous *precedent* that would inevitably lead to greater taxes, so "it was necessary they should oppose it, in its first stage of execution."

Paine also noted that many Americans did not voice their opposition to the Stamp Act in terms of well-reasoned general principles. There "were many, who, with best intentions, did not choose the best, nor indeed the true ground, to defend their cause upon. They felt themselves right by a general impulse, without being able to separate, and analyze, and arrange the parts."

Paine's reference to "a general impulse" is key to understanding the colonial mentality. Revolutionary Americans *felt*, on a gut level, the inestimable value of individual freedom and the dangers of government power—a feeling that was articulated in writing by Paine, Jefferson, Adams, and other libertarian authors. Without that fundamental, ingrained, and widespread *sentiment* of freedom, the writings of American revolutionaries would have had few if any practical consequences.

So have I answered my previous question? Have I explained what libertarians can find to celebrate in Independence Day? Yes and no. There was much in colonial America (slavery in particular) that was ugly—but there was also the ideal of freedom that, however compromised in practice, was sincerely believed, felt, and acted upon by a significant portion of the population. This tells us, at the very least, that the ideal of individual freedom is more than a will-o'-the-wisp, that it was widely appreciated in the past and so may become widely appreciated in the future.

I'm not sure if all this is cause for celebration, but certainly it is cause for hope. Such nuances, however, are irrelevant to my life. If to celebrate means to goof off, then I will always celebrate the Fourth of July with the enthusiasm of a fanatical patriot.

PART 1

History of the American Revolution

1

Americans with Attitudes: Smuggling in Colonial America

Since the 17th century, American commerce had been regulated by a complex system of British laws. The basic idea behind this "mercantile system," as Adam Smith called it—or "mercantilism," as it was later called—was fairly simple. The colonies were to produce raw materials, many of which could be shipped only to Britain, and Britain, in turn, would produce finished products to sell to the colonies.

During the 1720s and 1730s, while Robert Walpole was the English prime minister, many of the trade laws were loosely enforced, if at all. Walpole's motto, "Let sleeping dogs lie," was reflected in his attitude toward the American colonies. A free-trader at heart, Walpole allowed the Board of Trade, the enforcement arm of mercantilism, to languish. And to the important position of Secretary of State for the Southern Department, Walpole appointed the like-minded Thomas Pelham, Duke of Newcastle.

The Duke of Newcastle was responsible for American affairs. More interested in the patronage of his office than in enforcing commercial regulations, Newcastle pursued a policy that the Irish statesman Edmund Burke later called "salutary neglect." That is to say, Newcastle pretty much left the colonies alone, allowing customs officials to take bribes in exchange for looking the other way. In the view of Burke and other proponents of free trade, this neglect—or "corruption," as some called it—allowed both Americans and Britons to prosper. It was said that Newcastle had a closet-full of unopened dispatches from colonial governors who were complaining about American lawlessness.

As a result of salutary neglect, smuggling was rampant in the colonies, and most Americans saw nothing wrong with it. They did not look kindly on government interference with their commercial activities. They agreed with Thomas Jefferson that free trade is a "natural right."

For example, in 1756 and 1757, some 400 chests of tea were imported into Philadelphia, but only 16 were imported legally. Indeed, three-quarters or more of the tea consumed by Americans was illegal. In 1763, the British government estimated the value of commodities smuggled into the colonies at 700,000 pounds annually, an enormous sum at that time.

The preference for inexpensive tea was not peculiar to Americans. Over half the tea consumed in England was smuggled, and English smugglers, like their American counterparts, could get quite indignant when their free-trade activities were interrupted by government. Consider this reaction of an English smuggler when his vessel was boarded and his men arrested by Captain Bursack of the *Speedwell*, a British revenue cutter. The captain of the smugglers was not aboard when this happened, but he made his feelings known in a letter to Captain Bursack:

> Sir: Damn thee and God damn thy two purblind eyes thou bugger, thou death-looking son of a bitch. O, that I had been there (with my company) for thy sake when thou tookest them men of mine on board the Speedwell cutter on Monday, the 14th of December. I would drove thee and thy gang to Hell where thou belongest, thou Devil incarnet. Go down,

thou Hell Hound, unto they kennel below and bathe thyself in that sulphurous lake that has been so long prepared for such as thee, for it is time the world was rid of such a monster. Thou art no man but a devil, thou fiend. O Lucifer, I hope thou will soon fall into Hell like a star from the sky, there to lie unpitied and unrelented of any for ever and ever, which God grant of his infinite mercy. Amen.

The period of salutary neglect came to an end during the Seven Years' War (1756–1763)—known in America as the French and Indian War—when many American merchants engaged in trade with the French. Trading with the enemies of Britain during wartime was something of a tradition among the colonials. During an earlier war, for instance, American merchants used neutral ports in the Caribbean to exchange their provisions for French molasses, while bribing customs officers to obtain false clearance papers.

One method of trading with the enemy was especially popular in Rhode Island, the smuggling capital of America. Flags of truce were used to exchange prisoners, and merchants found that these could be purchased at reasonable prices from colonial governors. Then, after hiring some men who spoke French to pose as prisoners, and sailing under flags of truce,

American merchants traded with the French West Indies. In 1748, an American wrote to a correspondent in Amsterdam:

> The sweets of the French trade by way of flags of truce has put me upon turning my navigation that way, which is the most profitable business I know of. But, my friend, of this you must not lisp a word.

This illegal trade continued during the Seven Years' War, especially during its later phase when inhabitants of the French West Indies were desperate for food. Merchants from Newport, Boston, New York, Philadelphia, and other ports carried foodstuffs to the enemy for handsome profits.

Pennsylvania's wartime governor, William Denny, conducted a brisk trade in flags of truce. He sold so many that by 1759, the flags were traded openly on the New York market.

This wartime commerce with the enemy infuriated British military commanders, but it was difficult to stop. Smugglers were typically acquitted by sympathetic American juries, and informing on a smuggler could prove dangerous. When a New Yorker wrote an article that implicated two justices of New York's Supreme Court in the nefarious traffic, newspapers refused to print it. Then the informer was hauled in a cart through the streets, pelted with filth, and thrown in jail.

Americans continued their smuggling ways after the close of the Seven Years' War in 1763. An English writer commented on the widespread violation of trade laws:

> It was a matter of astonishment to observe what little care was taken to enforce the laws. The breaches openly committed against the Acts of Trade, and the shameful prostitution of office which prevailed in most of the ports on the Continent, could not escape the notice of the most superficial observer. The merchants had commonly undertaken these voyages which afforded the greatest prospect of gain, without any further regard to their illegality than that the Custom House must be silenced, by what means was but too obvious.

The loyalist Peter Oliver, former Chief Justice of the Superior Court of Massachusetts, recalled with horror how religious and upstanding merchants smuggled with a clear conscience. One prominent merchant, after sailing his ship full of contraband into Boston Harbor, would appear at the customhouse before it opened in the morning. He would raise a hand and swear that anything else he swore that day would be untrue. Then, after the customhouse opened for business, this merchant would swear before an officer that his contraband-laden ship contained no contraband.

Oliver related how another merchant solved the problem of swearing under oath that he was not smuggling:

> Another Captain boasted, that he had evaded the law, by writing two manifests of his cargo, one of which contained the contraband goods he had on board, and in the other manifest those goods were left out. He then went to the customhouse and stuck the true manifest in the sleeve of that hand which he was to hold up in swearing, and delivered the false manifest to the Officer, and swore the manifest to be a true one, meaning that which was in his sleeve.

In 1763, Prime Minister George Grenville cracked down on bribery and illicit trade. Eight warships and twelve armed sloops were sent to patrol American waters and pull in smugglers. Previously, many customs officers had remained in England while sending low-paid underlings to America to do the dirty work. Grenville ordered these officers to take up their posts in America or resign. They would be fired immediately if they neglected their duties.

Grenville was just getting started. Customs duties had been designed to regulate the flow of trade, not to raise revenue. Indeed, the trade laws cost four times more to enforce than they brought in, so Grenville set to work on a long list of proposals to raise revenue and curtail smuggling. In 1764, Parliament enacted these proposals, commonly called the Sugar Act, into law.

Six sections of the Sugar Act dealt with new taxes, and over 40 additional sections were devoted to far-reaching changes in commercial regulations, including rigorous methods of enforcement. These regulations were a bureaucratic nightmare that greatly increased the cost of doing business and, in some cases, made compliance for merchants engaged in inter-colonial trade nearly impossible. Any small vessel engaged in inland trade would probably be guilty of some violation or other, even when there was no criminal intent. This left the door open for racketeering by customs officers who lined their pockets by seizing vessels for technical violations.

The Sugar Act facilitated this abuse by implementing new guidelines for prosecuting accused smugglers. The owner of a seized vessel had to pay the cost of his trial in advance or forfeit everything. Even if he was exonerated, the owner could not recover these court costs. Nor could he sue a customs officer, so long as the judge certified that the sei-zure had been made with probable cause. To make matters worse, the government did not have to present evidence of fraud. The owner was presumed guilty and had to prove his innocence.

Armed with these legal weapons, some customs officers declared open season on American commerce. Such was the case with the rapacious Daniel Moore, collector of customs for Charleston. Moore harassed small merchants in South Carolina ports. When some merchants sued Moore and won, he vowed revenge, declaring that he would "sweat the merchants at law with their own money."

Moore was as good as his word. He seized a small vessel, the *Active*, and dragged its owner into a vice-admiralty court, which operated without a jury. The owner of the *Active* was cleared of all charges. But Moore, according to the judge, had seized the vessel with probable cause, so the owner was assessed court costs in the amount of 150 pounds—nearly double the value of the vessel itself. This is what Moore meant by sweating merchants at law with their own money.

Even rigorous enforcement of the Sugar Act could not always shield customs officers from the wrath of irate Americans. This was especially true in Rhode Island, where, unlike most other colonies, the governor was elected by popular vote, not appointed by the Crown. Moreover, when a customs officer caught a smuggler red-handed, the smuggler had to face a judge and prosecuting attorney who were native Rhode Islanders—men sympathetic to the cause of free trade. The judge might call a trial on short notice when he knew the customs officer was far away and unable to testify, thereby resulting in a dismissal for lack of evidence. Or if a judge had no choice but to convict a smuggler and confiscate his ship, he might later sell the vessel back to the smuggler for a fraction of its true value. But the simplest way to keep the wheels of commerce turning was to grease the eagerly outstretched palms of customs officers.

As these and many similar examples illustrate, Americans who had grown accustomed to decades of salutary neglect deeply resented the post-war efforts of the British government to impose taxes—especially when those taxes were raised for the express purpose of maintaining 10,000 British troops in the colonies. As much as historians delight in tracing the influence of political philosophers, such as John Locke, on American thinking, there can be little doubt that no sophisticated ideological foundation was needed to motivate many Americans to evade British laws and even to resist their enforcement with violence.

So why did so many average Americans eventually leave their homes to fight against the British? One perspective was given by Captain Preston, an American who had fought the British at Concord on April 19, 1775. In 1842, this 91-year-old veteran was interviewed by a 21-year-old reporter. The young reporter apparently expected to hear stories of unjust taxes and oppression, and of revolutionaries schooled in theories of liberty. What he got was far different, and more to the point:

Reporter: "Captain Preston, did you take up arms against intolerable oppressions?"

Preston: "Oppression? I didn't feel them."

R: "What, were you not oppressed by the Stamp Act?"

P: "I never saw one of those stamps. I certainly never paid a penny for one of them."

R: "Well, what then about the tea tax?"

P: "I never drank a drop of the stuff; the boys threw it all overboard."

R: "Then I suppose you had been reading Harrington or Sidney or Locke about the eternal principles of liberty?"

P: "Never heard of 'em. We read only the Bible, the Catechism, Watts' Psalms, and the Almanac."

R: "Well, then, what was the matter? And what did you mean in going to this fight?"

P: "Young man, what we meant in going for those redcoats was this: We always had governed ourselves, and we always meant to. They didn't mean we should."

2

"Liberty and Property!" The Sons of Liberty and Resistance to the Stamp Act

The Stamp Act, which sailed through Parliament and received the king's approval on March 22, 1765, was essentially a tax on paper goods. It required various legal and commercial documents to be printed on special paper that had been stamped, or embossed, by the Treasury Office in England, The items taxed included documents used in court proceedings, insurance policies, licenses to practice law, deeds, leases, mortgages, bonds, contracts, bills of lading, customs clearances, playing cards, pamphlets, almanacs, and newspapers.

Americans learned of the Stamp Act in April 1765, seven months before it was scheduled to go into effect. Grumblings were heard here and there, but no one grumbled more effectively than a 29-year-old Virginian named Patrick Henry.

Patrick Henry was a member of the Virginia House of Burgesses. The upstart leader of a radical minority, Henry waited until most of his fellow legislators had left for home at the end of May. Then, with only 39 of 116 members present, Henry pushed through five resolves that condemned the Stamp Act and affirmed American rights.

Patrick Henry's fifth resolve denied Parliament's right to tax the colonies. The legislature later rescinded this resolution and erased all mention of it from the official record. But word was out. The resolves were circulated in other colonies and printed in newspapers, appearing first in the *Newport Mercury*.

The *Mercury* printed all the resolves without mentioning that the fifth had been rescinded. It also printed a mysterious sixth resolve, suggesting that it, too, had been adopted by the Virginia legislature. The fictional sixth resolve sanctioned disobedience:

Resolved, that his Majesty's Liege People, the Inhabitants of this Colony, are not bound to yield Obedience to any Law of Ordinance whatever, designed to impose any Taxation whatsoever upon them, other than the Laws or Ordinances of the General Assembly aforesaid.

Confusion intensified when the *Maryland Gazette* published its version of the Virginia Resolves. It added a seventh resolution to the growing list:

Resolved, that any Person who shall, by Speaking or Writing, assert or maintain, That any Person or Persons, other than the General Assembly of this Colony, with such Consent as aforesaid, have any Right or Authority to lay or impose any Tax whatever on the Inhabitants thereof, shall be deemed, AN ENEMY TO THIS HIS MAJESTY'S COLONY.

As newspapers throughout the colonies reprinted the Virginia Resolves, they mistakenly included the sixth and seventh resolutions as though they had been adopted by the Virginia legislature. This was apparently owing to the efforts of Patrick Henry and his allies. When the conservative editor of the *Virginia Gazette* had refused to print even the authentic resolves, this left no reliable account from which other newspapers could draw. Henry and his friends filled the void.

They distributed their expanded version of the Virginia Resolves, and this version wound its way through the colonies. The physician David Ramsay described the tremendous influence of the Virginia Resolves:

> They circulated extensively, and gave a spring to the discontented. Till they appeared, most were of the opinion, that the [Stamp] Act would be quietly adopted. Murmurs, indeed, were common, but they seemed to be such as would soon die away. The countenance of so respectable a colony as Virginia confirmed the wavering and emboldened the timid. Opposition to the Stamp Act, from that period, assumed a bolder face. The fire of liberty blazed forth from the press. The flame spread from breast to breast, till the conflagration became general.

The Stamp Act was hard on printers of newspapers, pamphlets, and almanacs. In addition to imposing a tax on newspapers themselves, it imposed heavy taxes on advertisements. Moreover, newspapers printed in any language other than English had to pay double the normal rate. This was a veritable decree of bankruptcy for German printers in Philadelphia.

Threatened with economic distress, many printers rallied in opposition to the Stamp Act. As David Ramsay remarked:

> Printers, when uninfluenced by government, have generally arranged themselves on the side of liberty, nor are they less remarkable for attention to the profits of their profession. A stamp duty, which openly invaded the first, and threatened the last, provoked their united and zealous opposition.

Among the colonial newspapers protesting the Stamp Act, one stood out: the *Boston Gazette*, printed by Benjamin Edes and John Gill. Governor Bernard of Massachusetts assailed the *Gazette* as "the most factious paper in America," and he called a major contributor, James Otis, "perhaps as wicked a man as lives."

As we have seen, many Americans erroneously believed that Virginia had called for resistance against the Stamp Act. The legislature of Rhode Island followed this false lead and endorsed resistance, but it was the only colonial assembly to go this far. The resistance movement against the Stamp Act arose not from colonial legislatures but from the press and extra-legal organizations calling themselves "Sons of Liberty."

Unlike trade laws, the Stamp Act could not be evaded through smuggling. How, then, could Americans oppose it? One way was to boycott British goods until Parliament repealed the detested law. But organizing a nonimportation movement took time, so Americans searched for other ways to keep the Stamp Act from going into effect.

Radicals arrived at an ingenious and violent solution. They would pressure the stamp distributors to resign their offices. Thus, without a way to distribute stamped paper, the government could not collect its taxes. The town of Boston spearheaded this strategy.

When Bostonians awoke on August 14, 1765, they found an effigy, dressed in rags, hanging from a huge elm tree at the intersection of Essex and Orange streets. The effigy represented Andrew Oliver, the stamp distributor and brother-in-law of Massachusetts lieutenant governor Thomas Hutchinson. This effigy, Governor Bernard reported, could not be removed:

> Some of the neighbors offered to take it down, but they were given to know that would not be permitted. The Sheriff reported, that his officers had endeavored to take down the effigy, but could not do it without imminent danger to their lives.

Later that day, a crowd of tradesmen cut down the effigy and carried it to the wharves at Boston's south end, to the site of an unfinished building owned by Andrew Oliver. The protesters assumed (mistakenly) that this was the office from which Oliver planned to distribute stamps, so they engaged in a form of protest known as "pulling down the house." This took less than 30 minutes.

The crowd then gathered the timber from Oliver's building and carried it, along with the effigy, to Oliver's home at the foot of Fort Hill. There, they ceremoniously beheaded the effigy and not-so-ceremoniously threw rocks through Oliver's windows.

Next, the protesters ascended Fort Hill, and, to further emphasize their displeasure with the Stamp Act, they "stamped" their feet on what remained of Oliver's effigy and burned it in a bonfire made, appropriately enough, of the wood from Oliver's former building. Then it was back down the hill to Oliver's house once again. By now, however, the stamp distributor and his family had wisely found sanctuary in a neighbor's home. Governor Bernard told what happened next:

> The mob, finding the doors barricaded, broke down the whole fence of the garden towards Fort Hill, and coming on beat in all the doors and windows of

the garden front, and entered the house. As soon as they had got possession, they searched about for Mr. Oliver, declaring they would kill him; finding that he had left the house, a party set out to search two neighboring houses, in one of which Mr. Oliver was, but happily they were diverted from this pursuit by a gentleman telling them, that Mr. Oliver was gone with the Governor to the Castle. Otherwise he would certainly have been murdered.

When Governor Bernard tried to call out drummers to alert the local militia, he was told that most of the drummers were probably in the mob. The governor then fled to the safety of Castle William in Boston Harbor. Later that night, Lieutenant Governor Hutchinson took matters in hand. Bernard described his fate:

After 11 O'Clock, the mob seeming to grow quiet, Lt. Governor Hutchinson and the Sheriff ventured to go to Mr. Oliver's house to endeavor to persuade them to disperse. As soon as they began to speak, a ringleader cried out, "The Governor and the Sheriff! To your arms, my boys!" Presently after a volley of stones followed, the two gentlemen narrowly escaped through favor of the night, not without some bruises.

The day after this riot, Andrew Oliver promised to resign his commission as Stamp Distributor.

On August 26, 12 days after the first riot, Boston witnessed another one. At dusk a huge crowd gathered around a bonfire on King Street. Shouting "Liberty and Property!" the mob split into two groups. One group made its way to the home of William Story, an official of the vice-admiralty court (which tried smugglers and other violators of trade laws). This group wrecked Story's house, plundered its contents, and burned official papers. The other group inflicted a similar fate on the home of Benjamin Hallowell, comptroller of customs.

The night was still young, so the two mobs combined forces and marched to the beautiful house of Thomas Hutchinson, lieutenant governor and chief justice of Massachusetts. Hutchinson described what happened:

> The hellish crew fell upon my house with the rage of devils and in a moment with axes split down the doors and entered. My son, being in the great entry, heard them cry, "Damn him, he is upstairs; we'll have him."

When the rioters discovered that Hutchinson had left, they set to work on his house and possessions. The destruction, as Hutchinson noted, was systematic and thorough:

> One of the best finished houses in the Province had nothing remaining but the bare walls and floors. Not contented with tearing off all the wainscot and hangings and splitting the doors to pieces, they beat down the partition wall; and although that alone cost them near two hours they cut down the cupola and they began to take the slate and boards from the roof and were prevented only by the approaching daylight from a total demolition of the building. The garden fence was laid flat, and all my trees broke down to the ground. Such ruins were never seen in America. Besides my plate and family pictures, household furniture of every kind, my own, my children and servant's apparel, they carried off about 900 sterling in money and emptied the house of everything whatsoever except a part of the kitchen furniture, not leaving a single book or paper in it, and have scattered or destroyed all the manuscripts and other papers I had been collecting for 30 years together besides a great number of public papers in my custody.

The leader of the Boston riots was Ebenezer McIntosh, a shoemaker and commander of Boston's south-end gang.

When McIntosh was arrested, some leading merchants informed the sheriff that should additional violence occur, no one would try to stop it. McIntosh was released.

Some other rioters were arrested, but a crowd entered the home of the jailer and compelled him to surrender the key. No one was ever punished for participating in the Boston riots.

News of the Boston riots spread quickly throughout the colonies. The Boston Sons of Liberty provided a strategic model that other colonies adopted to prevent the Stamp Act from being implemented. New organizations sprang up everywhere, and these Sons of Liberty used violence and threats of violence to pressure stamp distributors to resign.

The New York distributor, James McEvers, wished to avoid the fate of Boston's Andrew Oliver. McEvers explained that he could not risk losing his property:

> I have a large store of goods and seldom less than twenty-thousand pounds currency value in it with which the populace would make sad havoc. With respect to my own person I am not much concerned about it, but I must confess I am uneasy about my store, as a great part of what I have been laboring hard for is centered there.

McEvers resigned. The stamp distributors for New Jersey, New Hampshire, Virginia, and North Carolina followed suit. John Hughes, the distributor for Delaware and Pennsylvania, pledged he would not enforce the Stamp Act unless the other colonies did. In Georgia, George Angus managed to do his job for two weeks, after which he left for parts unknown.

Other distributors required more persuading. In Rhode Island, a mob burned an effigy of Augustus Johnston and ransacked his house. In Maryland, a mob pulled down the house of Zachariah Hood and forced him to flee the colony with only the clothes on his back. In South Carolina, two distributors fled for their lives. In Connecticut, Jared Ingersoll was accosted by a mob and told he would be lynched. All these men saw the light and resigned.

Resistance to the Stamp Act was not confined to the mainland colonies. In the Bahamas, the residents of New Providence informed the distributor that he would be buried alive if he failed to resign. After he refused, the crowd dug a grave and lowered a coffin into it. The distributor had second thoughts and yielded.

The Stamp Act was scheduled to go into effect on November 1, 1765. By that time, however, there were no distributors left in the 13 mainland colonies—except in Georgia, where (as noted previously) the distributor lasted only two weeks. The Sons of Liberty had been remarkably efficient.

Bells tolled on November 1, the official beginning of the Stamp Act, as Americans declared this to be a day of mourning. Violence was minimal, except in New York City, where the Sons of Liberty transported effigies of Lt. Governor Colden and the devil to Colden's house. After seizing Colden's carriage, the mob hanged the effigies and consigned them, along with the carriage, to a huge bonfire.

New Yorkers then turned their sights on Major Thomas James of the Royal Artillery. James had called the Sons of Liberty "a pack of rascals," claiming that he could drive them out of the city with two dozen men. The protesters stripped the major's house of its furnishings and used them to rekindle their patriotic bonfire.

Americans responded to the Stamp Act with more than mob violence. In October 1765, 27 men from nine colonies met in New York City to oppose the Stamp Act. Known as the Stamp Act Congress, this assembly was controlled by moderates, so it did not endorse violent resistance. But it did affirm some basic principles of the resistance movement:

> It is inseparably essential to the freedom of a people, and the undoubted right of Englishmen, that no

taxes should be imposed on them, but with their own consent, given personally, or by their representatives.

After asserting the principle of no taxation without representation, the Stamp Act Congress maintained that Americans could never be adequately represented in the British Parliament.

The people of these colonies are not, and from their local circumstances, cannot be represented in the House of Commons in Great Britain.

This claim was necessary because of a theoretical dispute that had emerged during the Stamp Act crisis. Defenders of the Stamp Act agreed that representation was a necessary precondition for taxation, but they also argued that Americans were in fact represented in Parliament—not actually, but *virtually*.

The doctrine of virtual representation was defended by Thomas Whately, secretary of the treasury under George Grenville. Whately wrote:

The fact is, that the inhabitants of the Colonies are represented in Parliament. They do not indeed choose the members of that assembly; neither are nine-tenths of the people of Britain electors. The Colonies are in exactly the same situation. All British subjects are really in the same situation; none are actually, all are virtually represented in Parliament. For every member of Parliament sits in the House, not as Representative of his own Constituents, but as one of that august assembly by which all of the Commons of Great Britain are represented.

Some Americans called for colonial representation in Parliament. As James Otis put it in *The Rights of the British Colonies Asserted and Proved:*

A representation in Parliament from the several colonies can't be thought an unreasonable thing, nor if asked, could it be called an immodest request. Besides the equity of an American representation in Parliament, a thousand advantages would result from it. It would be the most effectual means of giving those of both countries a thorough knowledge of each others interests; as well as that of the whole, which are inseparable.

This call for colonial representation was rejected by most American theorists, because they believed the colonies could never be adequately represented in Parliament. Sam Adams explained:

We are far from desiring any Representation in England, because we think the Colonies cannot be equally and fully represented; and if not equally then in effect not at all. A representative should be, and continue to be, well acquainted with the internal circumstance of the people whom he represents. Now the Colonies are at so great a distance from the place where Parliament meets, from which they are separated by a wide ocean; and their circumstances are so often and continually varying, as is the case with all countries not fully settled, that it would not be possible for men, though ever so well acquainted with them at the beginning of a Parliament, to continue to have an adequate knowledge of them during the existence of that Parliament.

Only American assemblies, according to Sam Adams, could fairly represent Americans. Therefore, only American assemblies could legitimately tax Americans. This argument became the dominant theme of the American resistance movement. The Stamp Act Congress declared:

The only representatives of the people of these colonies, are the persons chosen therein, by themselves; and no taxes ever have been, or can be constitutionally imposed on them, but by their respective legislatures.

In addition to riots and the Stamp Act Congress, Americans used yet another strategy to oppose the Stamp Act. Merchants from New York, Philadelphia, and Boston signed agreements to stop importing most British commodities. These nonimportation agreements paralyzed trade between Britain and the colonies. An English merchant reported:

> The present situation of the colonies alarms every person who has any connection with them. The avenues of trade are all shut up. We have no remittances, and are at our wit's end for want of money to fulfill our engagements with our tradesmen.

American merchants owed British creditors some four million pounds sterling, and many Americans suspended payments until the Stamp Act was repealed. An English politician noted the effectiveness of this tactic:

> The weapon with which the colonies armed themselves to most advantage, was the refusal of paying the debts they owed to our merchants at home, for goods and wares exported to the American provinces. These debts involved the merchants of London, Liverpool, Manchester, and other great trading towns, in a common cause with the Americans, who

forswore all traffic with us, unless the obnoxious Stamp Act was repealed.

British merchants pressured Parliament to repeal the Stamp Act, and Parliament did so in March 1766. At the same time, however, Parliament passed the Declaratory Act, which affirmed Parliament's right to pass laws and statutes sufficient to bind the people of America "in all cases whatsoever." This broad assertion of Parliamentary power—a theoretical face-saving device, so to speak—did nothing more than infuriate Americans even more. Radicals would repeatedly cite the Declaratory Act as evidence of Parliament's intent to reduce Americans "under absolute despotism," as the Declaration of Independence later put it.

Years later, in 1774, Edmund Burke, who had consistently opposed all attempts to tax the American colonies, delivered a brilliant speech before the House of Commons. Burke perceptively noted that theoretical appeals to parliamentary sovereignty would merely push Americans, who had a long tradition of freedom, closer to the edge of independence.

Do not burden [the Americans] by taxes; you were not used to do so from the beginning. Let this be your reason for not taxing. These are the arguments of states and kingdoms. Leave the rest to the schools; for there only they may be discussed with safety. But, if intemperately, unwisely, fatally, you sophisticate and poison the very source of government, by urging subtle deductions, and odious to those you govern, from the unlimited and illimitable nature of supreme sovereignty, you will teach them by these means to call that sovereignty itself in question. When you drive him hard, the boar will surely turn upon the hunters. If that sovereignty and their freedom cannot be reconciled, which will they take? They will cast your sovereignty in your face. Nobody will be argued into slavery.

3

A Misunderstanding, the Townshend Act, and More Trouble in the American Colonies

In 1767, the annual cost of maintaining the British army in the American colonies exceeded 400,000 pounds sterling. Parliament had repealed the Stamp Act the previous year, so, except for some minor revenues generated by the Sugar Act, English taxpayers were footing the bill.

These English taxpayers were growing restless. Already burdened with high taxes and a staggering debt from the Seven Years' War, they now faced new taxes on straw, canvas, linen, and other items. In addition, a huge land tax—another holdover from the war—compelled farmers to sell wheat at exorbitant prices. England was embroiled in a financial crisis, as food riots erupted throughout the land.

Many Englishmen resented the inequity of the tax system. The distinguished historian Robert Palmer estimated that taxes were 26 times higher in England than in America. Taxes in America were typically minimal—indeed, virtually nonexistent in some cases. (As Palmer quipped, "One suspects that 'no taxation without representation' meant no taxation with representation, either.") William Johnson, an American residing in England, commented on the disparity.

> Great pains have been taken to irritate the people of England against America, especially the freeholders, and to persuade them that they are to pay infinite taxes and we none; they are to be burdened that we may be eased; and, in a word, that the interests of Britain are to be sacrificed to those of America.

Despite the failure of the Stamp Act, Charles Townshend, chancellor of the exchequer, decided to tax the colonies again. In the summer of 1767, he pushed the Townshend Revenue

Act through Parliament. This act levied new import duties on all glass, paper, paint, and tea entering the colonies.

The Townshend Act breezed through Parliament. Even previous opponents of the Stamp Act nodded their approval, and there was little concern that the new taxes (which were quite small) would provoke resistance in America.

This complacency seems curious, considering the fierce resistance to the Stamp Act just two years earlier. Why did British politicians think Americans would accept the new taxes? To understand the reason for this assumption, we need to understand a fundamental misunderstanding that emerged about the American position on taxation—a misunderstanding that was unintentionally aggravated by Benjamin Franklin, who was in London representing American interests at the time.

Most Americans distinguished between trade regulations and taxes. Parliament, these Americans believed, *did* have a right to regulate American trade, but Parliament did *not* have a right to levy taxes in America without the consent of colonial assemblies. Taxes were specifically designed to generate revenue. Not so with the trade laws. Import duties might yield some revenue, but this was an incidental byproduct of their chief function, which was to regulate commerce.

Benjamin Franklin summarized this distinction when he testified before Parliament in 1766, during a hearing on the Stamp Act. Here is how Franklin answered some of the questions put to him in a crucial and highly interesting exchange:

Member of Parliament (MP): Mr. Franklin, did you ever hear the authority of Parliament to make laws for America questioned till lately?

Franklin: The authority of Parliament was allowed to be valid in all laws, except such as should lay internal taxes. It was never disputed in laying duties to regulate commerce.

MP: What is your opinion of a future tax, imposed on the same principle with that of the Stamp Act? How would Americans receive it?

Franklin: Just as they do this [i.e., the Stamp Act]. They would not pay it.

MP: Have you not heard of the resolutions of this House [of Commons], and of the House of Lords, asserting the right of Parliament relating to America, including a power to tax the people there?

Franklin: Yes, I have heard of such resolutions.

MP: What will be the opinion of the Americans on those resolutions?

Franklin: They will think them unconstitutional and unjust.

MP: Was it an opinion in America before 1763 that the Parliament had no right to lay taxes and duties there?

Franklin: I never heard any objection to the right of laying duties to regulate commerce; but a right to lay internal taxes was never supposed to be in Parliament, as we are not represented there.

So far, Franklin had accurately represented the American position. He denied Parliament's right to tax the colonies, while conceding its right to levy duties for regulating trade. Later, however, confusion set in when a hostile MP pressed Franklin to defend this distinction:

MP: Mr. Franklin, you say the colonies have always submitted to external taxes, and object to the right of Parliament only in laying internal taxes. Now can you show that there is any kind of difference between the two taxes to the colony on which they may be laid?

Franklin: I think the difference is very great. An external tax is a duty laid on commodities imported; that duty is added to the first cost and other charges on the commodity and, when it is offered for sale, makes a part of the price. If the people do not like it at that price, they refuse it; they are not obliged to pay it. But an internal tax is forced from the people without their consent, if not laid by their own representatives.

Here, Franklin distinguished between two kinds of taxes: internal and external. The Stamp Act imposed *internal* taxes, whereas import duties were *external* taxes. According to Franklin, Americans opposed internal but not external taxes. This was a very misleading way of putting the matter. Although Franklin correctly noted American acceptance of import duties (in theory, if frequently not in practice), in dubbing these duties "external taxes," Franklin inadvertently facilitated passage of the Townshend Act.

Franklin's testimony left a lasting impression on members of Parliament, persuading them that Americans would pay taxes so long as those taxes were "external"—that is, so long as they were collected through import duties. Charles Townshend regarded the distinction between internal and external taxes as absurd, but if Americans wished to draw this distinction, so be it. As Townshend informed Parliament:

> I do not know any distinction between internal and external taxes; it is a distinction without a difference. It is perfect nonsense. If we have a right to impose one, we have the other. Yet since Americans are pleased to make that distinction, I am willing to indulge them and choose for that reason to confine myself to regulations of trade, by which a sufficient revenue might be raised in America.

This is why the Townshend Revenue Act passed without significant parliamentary opposition. Even many of America's "friends" in Parliament believed that the Townshend duties merely imposed the kind of external taxes that Benjamin Franklin said Americans would pay without protest.

Parliament had been badly misinformed on this issue. Most American spokesmen rejected *all* taxation by Parliament, both internal *and* external. True (as I noted previously), Americans conceded Parliament's right to levy import duties, but they conceded this right only for the purpose of regulating trade, not for the purpose of raising revenue—and the Townshend duties were expressly designed to raise revenue.

Predictably, therefore, Americans opposed the Townshend Revenue Act. Late in 1767, the American lawyer John Dickinson presented the basic objections in *Letters from a Farmer in Pennsylvania*—the most popular and influential pamphlet in America prior to the publication, eight years later, of Thomas Paine's *Common Sense*. Dickinson set the record straight. Americans opposed all taxes levied by Parliament, internal and external:

> It is said that the duties imposed by the Stamp Act were *internal* taxes, but the present [Townshend duties] are *external*, and therefore the Parliament may have a right to impose them. With this I answer with a total denial of the power of Parliament to lay upon these colonies any "tax" whatever.

Dickinson continued with an argument that would become extremely important to the American resistance movement, a point that would be repeated time and again in future conflicts. As an attorney schooled in English common law, Dickinson clearly understood the legal significance of *precedents*, so he insisted that unjust taxes must be opposed at the outset, regardless of the amount of money involved.

Some persons may think this act of no consequence, because the duties are so small. *That* is the very circumstance most alarming to me. For I am convinced that the authors of this law would never have obtained an act to raise so trifling a sum as it must do, had they not intended by *it* to establish a *precedent* for future use. To console ourselves with the smallness of the duties is to walk deliberately into the snare that is set for us, praising the *neatness* of the workmanship.

In short, if they have a right to levy a tax of one penny upon us, they have a right to levy a *million* upon us: For where does their right stop?

Americans feared the Townshend Act for another reason: revenues raised from it were to be used to pay the salaries of colonial governors and judges. This proposal struck at the heart of a revered American tradition. Although the Crown appointed governors in 11 colonies, their salaries were paid by the colonial legislatures. This "power of the purse" enabled American assemblies to check the power of governors and judges by withholding their salaries.

The Townshend Act sought to overthrow this traditional safeguard by releasing governors and judges of their financial dependence on colonial legislatures, and this alarmed many Americans. As Dickinson put it:

> No free people ever existed, or can ever exist, without keeping, to use a common but strong expression, "the purse strings." Where this is the case, they have a constitutional check upon the administration, which may thereby be brought into order without violence. But where such a power is not lodged in the people, oppression proceeds uncontrolled in its career, till the governed, transported into a rage, seek redress in the midst of blood and confusion.

Other provisions in the Townshend Act cracked down on smuggling. A board of customs commissioners was sent to America to oversee enforcement of the trade laws. These commissioners were not well received when they arrived in Boston. Joseph Harrison, collector for the port of Boston, described the hostile atmosphere:

> A dangerous and seditious combination has been formed to resist the execution of those Acts of Parliament and indeed of all others that impose any duties payable in the colonies. In order to effect this the newspapers have been employed all this last winter in circulating a vast number of inflaming and seditious

publications tending to poison and incense the minds of the people and alienate them from all regard and obedience to the legislature of the Mother Country. A general discontent began to prevail and soon showed itself by an almost universal clamor against all duties, customs and customhouse officers: even the penny a gallon duty on molasses is now found out to be oppressive and illegal: the common cry being, "Pay no duties! Save your money and you save your country!" so that running of goods and smuggling is become public virtue and patriotism.

Brutal punishment was sometimes meted out to customs officers after passage of the Townshend Act. When a minor customs officer in Philadelphia, William Shepherd, tried to confiscate smuggled Madeira wine, his life was threatened. Refusing to be intimidated, Shepherd ventured out on the streets of Philadelphia after dark. He described what happened next:

Upon my return home about a quarter past ten o'clock, two men of a sudden came up to me. One of them without saying a word to me, struck me as hard as he could in the pit of my stomach, which immediately deprived me of breath and I fell down. He took the advantage with some weapon, I apprehend a knife, and slit my nose. I suppose his intention was to slit it up to my eyes. He did not altogether succeed in this, though he did in part, having cut the inside thereof considerably and more than a quarter of an inch clear through. I received several blows upon my face, which bruised it greatly and cause a large swelling.

After this assault Shepherd wanted nothing more than to quit his job and return to England. He was sick to death of dealing with hostile and unruly Americans.

I could not think of tarrying among a set of people, under my present circumstances, whose greatest pleasure would be to have an opportunity of burying me. The few acquaintances that I had in Philadelphia were afraid of being seen to keep company with me, so I was in a manner alone in the city without a friend to assist me in any trouble. I was obliged to confine myself at home at night, as I did not know what murderous intentions the people had determined to execute against me. As I passed through the streets, I was the object that everyone stared and gazed at. I at present think myself unable to persevere any longer in Philadelphia.

4

The Boston Massacre

Events in Boston were getting out of hand. On June 10, 1768, the *Liberty*, a sloop owned by John Hancock, was seized for illegally importing Madeira wine. (Hancock, a wealthy man, eventually accumulated around 500 indictments for smuggling.) Angry Bostonians responded by assaulting the customs officers. One of these officers, Benjamin Harrison, told the story:

We were pursued by the mob which by this time was increased to a great multitude. The onset was begun by throwing dirt at me, which was presently succeeded by volleys of stones, brickbats, sticks or anything else that came to hand. In this manner I ran the gauntlet of near 200 yards, my poor son following behind endeavoring to shelter his father by receiving the strokes of many of the stones, till at length he became equally an object of their resentment, was knocked down and then laid hold of by the legs, arms, and hair of his head, and in that manner dragged along in a most barbarous and cruel manner.

I received a violent blow on the breast which had like to have brought me to the ground, and I verily believe if I had fallen, I should never have got up again, the people to all appearance being determined on blood and murder.

This incident convinced Commodore Hood of the Royal Navy that Boston was on the brink of revolt. Hood wrote to his superiors in London:

What has been so often foretold is now come to pass. The good people of Boston seem ready and ripe for open revolt, and nothing, it is imagined, can prevent it but immediate armed force.

General Gage, Commander-in-Chief of British forces in America, was of a similar mind. He wrote to the government:

If a determined resolution is taken to enforce at all events a due submission to that dependence on the

parent state, to which all Colonies have been sub-
jected, you can not act with too much vigor. Quash
this spirit at a blow, without too much regard to the
expense, and it will prove economy in the end.

Rumors circulated of plans to garrison soldiers in Boston, and
for once, rumors had understated the case. Almost the entire
British garrison stationed in Halifax (Nova Scotia)—around
700 soldiers—arrived in Boston in September 1768, and an
additional 1,000 soldiers were on their way from Ireland.

As British warships sailed into Boston Harbor, they lined
up in a menacing battle formation, their broadsides facing
the town. Bostonians were hostile but restrained. Local officials refused to provide quarters for the troops, so the British
rented various buildings scattered throughout Boston. This
was asking for trouble. The brutal punishments inflicted by
British officers on common soldiers made desertions a constant threat; and now, without a central barracks or bivouac
where the soldiers could be watched, they began deserting at
an alarming rate—around 70 in the first two weeks alone.

Consequently, the British tried to seal off Boston to prevent
their own troops from escaping. Sentinels were ordered to
keep a sharp watch, and they faced hundreds of lashes if they
let a deserter slip by. At night, sentinels challenged passersby,

who were supposed to respond by shouting "Friend!" Few Bostonians were willing to play this game, so tempers flared as civilians confronted soldiers.

Sam Adams was outraged by the military presence in his town:

> When these sentinels call upon everyone who passes by, to know Who comes there?, as the phrase is, I take it to be in the highest degree impertinent, unless they can show a legal authority for doing so. There is something in it, which looks like the town was altogether under the government and control of the military power. And as long as the inhabitants are fully persuaded that this is not the case at present, and moreover hope and believe that it never will be, it has a natural tendency to irritate the minds of all who have a just sense of honor, and think they have the privilege of walking the streets without being controlled.

The civil rights of Bostonians were in jeopardy. Some responded by affirming their right to bear arms in self-defense. One anonymous Bostonian declared:

> It is a natural right which the people have reserved to themselves to keep arms for their own defense, and it is to

be made use of when the sanctions of society and law are found insufficient to restrain the violence of government.

Bostonians were getting touchy, to say the least, but they had reason to cheer on August 1, 1769, when Governor Bernard sailed for England, never to return. Bostonians were not exactly sorry to see the Governor go, as they indicated by posting broadsides with this farewell poem:

Go, Bernard, thou minion! To thy country go,
For Boston, loud proclaims you freedom's foe.
Go on, ye pilferer, with all the rage
That half-starved spaniels for a bone engage.
Go join in concert with the croaking frogs,
Or howl in chorus with a pack of dogs;
With monkeys go and chatter on a stage,
Or turn a mastiff and each cur engage.
Better, do worse! Turn panderer, pimp, or slave,
Turn highwayman, turn murderer, or knave.

The military occupation of Boston caused many problems and solved none. By the summer of 1769, this was apparent even to General Gage:

The people were as lawless and licentious after the troops arrived as they were before. They were there contrary to the wishes of the Council, Assembly, Magistrates, and People, and seemed only offered to abuse and ruin.

Two regiments were withdrawn from Boston, but two remained. Scuffles between soldiers and civilians become more frequent, and tragedy struck on the evening of March 5, 1770. A scuffle escalated and ended in the death of five Bostonians.

Eyewitnesses gave conflicting accounts of the Boston Massacre (as Americans dramatically called it), but the subsequent trial spoke well for American justice. The British officer in charge, Captain Preston, was defended by John Adams and acquitted by an American jury.

Sam Adams (a distant cousin of John Adams) disagreed with the verdict, but he believed there was a more important issue involved. Incidents like the Boston Massacre were bound to occur whenever soldiers were garrisoned with civilians.

Bostonians wanted the soldiers out of Boston. Thomas Hutchinson, the acting governor, partially complied. He withdrew one of the two remaining regiments to Castle William in Boston Harbor. This wasn't good enough for the Americans, however, so Sam Adams paid a visit to the governor. If Hutchinson had the power to remove one regiment,

Adams bluntly declared, then he had the power to remove the other regiment. Adams issued a thinly veiled threat:

> It is at your peril if you refuse. The meeting is composed of 3000 people. They are become impatient. A thousand men are already arrived in the neighborhood, and the whole country is in motion. Night is approaching. An immediate answer is expected. Both regiments or none.

Thomas Hutchinson capitulated to avoid "a perfect convulsion," and Boston was spared additional violence.

From 1771 to 1783, annual orations were given in Massachusetts to commemorate the Boston Massacre. These typically included condemnations of standing armies—that is, professional armies maintained in peacetime. Opposition to standing armies had long been an important element of Radical Whig ideology—a political philosophy that animated the American resistance movement—and the Boston Massacre reinforced this traditional hostility. Consider this passage from the oration given in 1772 by Dr. Joseph Warren, a resistance leader who was later killed at the Battle of Bunker Hill:

> Soldiers are taught to consider arms as the only arbiters by which every dispute is to be decided between

contending states. They are instructed implicitly to obey their commanders, without inquiring into the justice of the cause they are engaged to support; hence it is, that they are ever to be dreaded as the ready engines of tyranny and oppression.

Most Americans regarded citizen militias, not standing armies, as the proper way to defend a free society. The Boston merchant John Hancock made this point in his 1774 memorial oration:

Since standing armies are so hurtful to a state, perhaps my countrymen may demand some substitute, some other means of rendering us secure against the incursions of a foreign enemy. But can you be one moment at a loss? Will not a well disciplined militia afford you ample security against foreign foes? From a well regulated militia we have nothing to fear; their interest is the same with that of the state. They do not jeopardize their lives for a master who considers them only as the instruments of his ambition and whom they regard only as the daily dispenser of the scanty pittance of bread and water. No, they fight for their houses, their lands, for their wives, their children, for all who claim the tenderest names, and are held dearest in their hearts. They fight for their liberty, for themselves, and for their God.

Ironically, March 5—the day of the Boston Massacre, a tragedy rooted in American resistance to the Townshend Act—was also the day when a new prime minister, Lord North, opened debate in Parliament on revising the Townshend duties. English merchants had petitioned for repeal because they were smarting from an American boycott.

Three positions emerged during the parliamentary debates. Some members, believing that the Townshend duties cost more in lost business than they brought in, favored total repeal. Hard-liners, on the other hand, opposed any changes whatsoever, arguing that any compromise would amount to a capitulation to American demands.

Lord North favored a middle course. He wanted to repeal all the Townshend duties except the duty on tea. This duty, which was quite small, should remain as a symbol of British authority and thereby reaffirm the right of Parliament to tax the American colonies.

Lord North got his way. On April 12, 1770, the Townshend duties on glass, paper, and paint were rescinded. Only the tax on tea was retained—a symbolic gesture that would later have profound and irreversible consequences.

5

The Coercive Acts and Their Theoretical Significance

The Boston Tea Party has often been called a pivotal event that led to the American Revolution, but it would be more accurate to say that the British response was the true catalyst.

Beginning in March 1774, in retaliation for the destruction of tea in Boston Harbor, Parliament passed four pieces of legislation known as the Coercive Acts. (Some historians include a fifth, the Quebec Act, among the Coercive Acts, but this had been in the works for some time and was not a direct response to the Boston Tea Party.) These measures, which many Americans called the Intolerable Acts, amounted to a declaration of martial law in Boston. They left Americans with no plausible course of action between the extremes of total submission and revolution.

The Coercive Acts closed the Port of Boston (with some minor exceptions) until Bostonians provided restitution to the East India Company, compensated customs officers for their losses, and showed proper respect for law and order. The charter of Massachusetts (its constitution, in effect) was severely altered to give the royal governor extensive powers. He could now appoint or fire "all judges of the inferior courts of common pleas, commissioners of oyer and terminer [i.e., judges who dealt with treason, felonies, and misdemeanors], the attorney general, provosts, marshals, justices of the peace, and other officers of the council or courts of justice." And "upon every vacancy of the offices of chief justice and judges of the superior court . . . the governor . . . shall have full power and authority to nominate and appoint the persons to succeed to the said offices, who shall hold their commissions during the pleasure of his Majesty."

Jurors would no longer be elected but instead would be appointed by sheriffs who served at the pleasure of the governor. Except for conducting routine business once a year, the Massachusetts Assembly was forbidden to meet without permission from the governor. Town meetings throughout

Massachusetts required similar permission to convene, and participants were forbidden to discuss anything that the governor deemed inappropriate.

In addition, a military governor, General Gage, replaced the civilian governor, Thomas Hutchinson, and Gage's authority would be backed by four regiments of British soldiers. (This was the same number—around 4,000, a ratio of one soldier to every four civilians—that had led to the Boston Massacre a few years earlier.) Civilians could be compelled to provide lodgings for these soldiers. And if a soldier or any officer of the Crown was accused of murder or other capital offense, his trial could be moved to England (or to another colony) at the discretion of the governor. It was with good reason that some Americans dubbed this last provision the "Murder Act."

The Tea Party had been universally excoriated by members of Parliament. Even those MPs known as "friends" of America called it a criminal act and demanded restitution for the East India Company. But some of these MPs vigorously protested the Coercive Acts as overkill. It was unfair, they said, to punish all Bostonians—indeed, all residents of Massachusetts—for the criminal actions of a small group. Moreover, the Coercive Acts would compel Americans to confederate in self-defense, and a full-scale revolution would probably be the result.

These were reasonable concerns—and accurate predictions, as it turned out—but most MPs were not in a reasonable mood. Indeed, one member went so far as to demand that Boston be burned and completely destroyed, as the Romans had done with Carthage.

The British Ministry had considered the possibility of bringing ringleaders of the Boston Tea Party to England for trial. The British had a list of the usual suspects, such as Samuel Adams and John Hancock, but they knew they had virtually no chance of finding witnesses who would testify against these popular resistance leaders. Prime Minister North therefore consoled himself with the belief that it was reasonable to punish the entire town of Boston, because that town "has been the ringleader of all violence and opposition to the execution of the laws of this country." In other words, the Coercive Acts were payback for much more than the Boston Tea Party.

Many prominent Americans also condemned the destruction of East India Company tea. Benjamin Franklin, writing before passage of the Coercive Acts, called the Tea Party "an act of violent injustice on our part," claiming that it was improper to destroy private property "in a dispute about public rights." Franklin feared the Tea Party would give the British an excuse to wage war against Americans, so he urged the

Massachusetts Assembly to indemnify the East India Company before Parliament retaliated.

George Washington was another American who condemned the destruction of tea, but his harsh reaction to the Coercive Acts illustrates their tremendous theoretical significance. The Coercive Acts fit perfectly into the conspiracy theory that some American radicals had been pushing since 1763, because those acts seemed to provide conclusive proof that the unjust actions of the British government over the past decade were not unrelated events. The Coercive Acts were viewed by many Americans as the culmination of a plan, or design, to extinguish American freedom and establish despotism.

As Washington wrote in letters to Bryan Fairfax (July and August, 1774), the Coercive Acts "made it as clear as the sun in its meridian brightness, that there is a regular, systematic plan formed to fix the right and practice of taxation among us." The British government "is pursuing a regular Plan at the expence of Law & justice, to overthrow our Constitutional Rights and liberties." This "fixed & uniform Plan" was designed to establish "the most despotick System of Tyranny that ever was practiced in a free Government. In short, what further proofs are wanting to satisfy one of the designs of the Ministry than their own Acts, which are uniform, & plainly tending to the same point." Washington was "convinc'd beyond the smallest doubt that these Measures [the Coercive Acts] are the result of deliberation."

To appreciate the theoretical significance of Washington's remarks, we need to recall this passage from the Declaration of Independence (my italics):

> Prudence, indeed, will dictate that governments long established should not be changed for light and transient causes; and accordingly all experience hath shown that mankind are more disposed to suffer, while evils are sufferable, than to right themselves by abolishing the forms to which they are accustomed. *But when a long train of abuses and usurpations, pursuing invariably the same object evinces a design to reduce them under absolute despotism, it is their right, it is their duty, to throw off such government, and to provide new guards for their future security.*

As I explained in an earlier chapter, a *design* to establish despotism was the bright line in Radical Whig ideology that separated the right of *resistance* from the right of *revolution*. Under certain conditions (which I will discuss in a later chapter), resistance against *specific* laws was viewed by Radical Whigs as justifiable, but revolution was another matter entirely. A revolution was not justified unless it could be shown that unjust laws were part of an overall *plan* to establish despotism. As John Locke put it in his *Second Treatise of Government* (1690):

> Revolutions happen not upon every little mismanagement in publick affairs. Great mistakes in the ruling part, many wrong and inconvenient Laws, and all the slips of human frailty will be born by the People, without mutiny or murmur. But if a long train of Abuses, Prevarications, and Artifices, all tending the same way, make the design visible to the people, and they cannot but feel, what they lie under, and see whither they are going; 'tis not to be wonder'd, that they should then rouze themselves, and endeavour to put the rule into such hands, which may secure to them the ends for which Government was at first erected.

George Washington was not alone in viewing the Coercive Acts as conclusive proof of a deliberate plan by the British government to establish despotism. Far from it; the same opinion was expressed many times by many Americans in letters, speeches, pamphlets, newspaper articles, and public documents.

According to the Boston Committee of Correspondence, the Coercive Acts were "glaring evidence of a fixed plan of the British administration to bring the whole continent into the most humiliating bondage." One orator spoke of the decision to station thousands of British troops in Boston as springing from a "PLAN . . . *systematically* laid, and pursued by the British *ministry*, near twelve years, for enslaving America." In *A Summary View of the Rights of British America* (1774), Thomas Jefferson wrote of the Coercive Acts:

> Scarcely have our minds been able to emerge from the astonishment into which one stroke of Parliamentary thunder has involved us, before another more heavy and more alarming is fallen on us. Single acts of tyranny may be ascribed to the accidental opinion of a day; but a series of oppressions, begun at a distinguished period, and pursued unalterably through every change of ministers, too plainly prove a deliberate, systematical plan of reducing us to slavery.

In the fall of 1774, John Adams, using the nom de plume *Novanglus*, published what was perhaps the most detailed account of how British politicians and American Tories had conspired for years to strip Americans of their rights and liberties. Throughout these essays, we find references to "a manifest design," "settled plans," "systematical means," and so forth.

The theoretical implications of the Coercive Acts were brilliantly summarized by Bernard Bailyn (*The Origins of American Politics*, 1967, pp. 11–12). Responding to those modern historians who had dismissed American claims of a British conspiracy as "extravagant, rhetorical, and apparently far from the realities of the time," Bailyn wrote:

> We shall have much disbelief to overcome. For what the leaders of the Revolutionary movement themselves said lay behind the convulsion of the time—what they themselves said was the cause of it—was nothing less than a deliberate "design"—a conspiracy—of ministers of state and their under-lings to overthrow the British constitution, both in England and in America, and to blot out, or at least severely reduce, English liberties. This undertaking, it was said, which had long been brewing, had been nourished in corruption—rank, festering corruption, rising from the inmost recesses of the English polity and coursing through every vein. What was happening in America through the 1760's, point by point in the controversy with England, could be seen, by the

end of that decade, as fitting a pattern of concerted malevolence familiar to every eighteenth-century student of history and politics. Britain, it was said, was following Greece, Rome, France, Venice, Denmark, Sweden—in fact almost the whole of continental Europe—from the liberty of a free constitution into autocracy, and the colonies, for reasons variously explained, were in the van. Individual details— Stamp Act, Townshend Duties, Boston Massacre, and ultimately and overwhelmingly the Coercive Acts—added up to something greater, more malevolent than their simple sum, which was finally and fully revealed in the substitution of military for civil actions in 1775.

6

Fingering the King on the Road to Independence

In the last chapter, I discussed how the Coercive Acts, which Parliament passed in retaliation for the Boston Tea Party, solidified the belief of many Americans that the British government had been planning for years "to reduce [Americans] under absolute despotism" (as Jefferson put it in the Declaration of Independence). This widespread belief in a British conspiracy had a spinoff effect—a fateful conclusion that was virtually necessitated by the inner logic of ideas.

Between the Stamp Act of 1765 and the Coercive Acts of 1774, the British ministry changed personnel a number of times. For example, the detested Stamp Act was repealed (March 1766) during the short-lived Rockingham administration, which enjoyed the support of Edmund Burke and other parliamentary "friends" of America. But at the same time that Parliament repealed the Stamp Act, it also passed the notorious Declaratory Act, according to which Parliament "had, hath, and of right ought to have, full power and authority to make laws and statutes of sufficient force and validity to bind the colonies and people of America . . . in all cases whatsoever."

The point of the Declaratory Act was to emphasize that Parliament repealed the Stamp Act as a favor, in effect, not on principle—and certainly not on the American principle of no taxation without representation. For many Americans, the Declaratory Act served as a constant reminder of the desire of Parliament to exercise unrestrained power over the colonies, so they naturally viewed each new encroachment on their rights as part of this overall plan. The Declaratory Act served as a recurring and unifying theme that linked various acts of Parliament into a continuous chain of conspiracy.

Some nagging questions remained, however: *Who* was behind this conspiratorial plan? Given the changing faces of various administrations, what was the *constant* factor that accounted for the unremitting efforts to subordinate Americans to the sovereignty of the British government in "all cases whatsoever"?

After passage of the Coercive Acts in 1774, one answer became increasingly common, namely: the *king* himself was the culprit. It was not some power behind the throne, but George III—the despot who sat on the throne—who had been at the center of the conspiracy all along. The king was the constant in a sea of variables.

Before 1774, most Americans, including many radicals, viewed George III as an unwitting dupe who was being manipulated by his corrupt, power-seeking advisers. Again and again, from the late 1760s to the early 1770s, Americans addressed fawning petitions to the king seeking redress for their grievances, but to no avail. Nevertheless, even the firebrand Samuel Adams attributed these failures to the "baneful Influence of corrupt and infamous Ministers and Servants of the Crown."

After George III approved the Coercive Acts (which was necessary for them to become law), the king rather than Parliament increasingly became the focus of attention and condemnation. It is difficult to overestimate the significance of this shift in perspective. To finger the king, to brand him a tyrant, was to abandon almost all hope of reconciliation and to run, not walk, to the precipice of revolution and, from there, to independence.

As one writer in the *Essex Gazette* explained, the Coercive Acts were the equivalent of a declaration of war against the colonies, and "if the King violates his sacred Faith to, and Compact with any one State of his Empire, he *discharges the same from their Allegiance to him, dismembers them from the Empire and reduces them to a State of Nature.*" In other words, he "CEASES TO BE THEIR KING."

To appreciate how radical this claim was, we need to understand the theory of allegiance that was being articulated by a growing number of Americans. According to this theory—which was defended by Benjamin Franklin, James Wilson, Thomas Jefferson, John Adams, and other prominent Americans—the colonies had *never* owed allegiance to the British Parliament. Legislatively considered, the colonies were autonomous states within the British Empire, and as such they owed allegiance *only* to the king. And this allegiance, in turn, was grounded in a mutual contract, according to which Americans pledged their allegiance in exchange for the king's protection.

This version of social contract theory stipulated that the king could continue to demand allegiance only so long as he fulfills his part of the agreement. If he violates his trust— as Americans believed he had with the Coercive Acts—he "unkings" himself and releases his subjects from their part of the deal. His subjects are thereby cast into a "state of nature"—that is, a society without government—and are then free to form a new government of their own choosing.

Silas Downer of Providence put this argument forcefully. In July 1774, Downer wrote to a friend: "The time is come . . . that we are independent. By the passing of the late Acts in the British Parliament, every Tye is cut, and we are set adrift." In September of the same year, during the First Continental Congress (which was convened in response to the Coercive Acts), Patrick Henry delivered a fiery speech that included these words:

> Government is dissolved. Fleets and armies and the present state of things show that government is dissolved. We are in a state of nature.

Historians sometimes refer to this position—which became even more common after serious fighting erupted at Lexington and Concord on April 19, 1775—as assertions of de facto independence. That is to say, the colonies were rendered independent, as a matter of *fact*, by the *king*, whose tyrannical decrees and behavior absolved his American subjects of any and all allegiance to him.

The significance of this argument for de facto independence can be seen in how it was used during the summer of 1776, as delegates to the Second Continental Congress debated the advisability of passing a formal declaration of independence. Some delegates from the middle colonies maintained that they could not vote for independence because they lacked authorization from their respective legislatures. In response, the radicals argued that independence was *already a fact* and that delegates did not need authorization to *acknowledge* a state of affairs that already existed.

Here is how Thomas Jefferson summarized this interesting argument in *Notes of Proceedings in the Continental Congress* (a document that Jefferson later inserted in his *Autobiography*). John Adams, Richard Henry Lee, George Wythe, and other radicals maintained

That the question was not whether, by a Declaration of Independence, we should make ourselves what we are not; but whether we should declare a fact which already exists.

That, as to the people or Parliament of England, we had always been independent of them . . . .

That, as to the King, we had been bound to him by allegiance, but that this bond was now dissolved by his assent to the last act of Parliament, by which he declares us out of his protection, and by his levying war on us, a fact which had long ago proved us out of his protection; it being a certain position in law, that allegiance and protection are reciprocal, the one ceasing when the other is withdrawn . . . .

No delegates then can be denied, or ever want, a power of declaring an existing truth.

This way of thinking, when combined with points I made earlier, helps us to understand some passages in the Declaration of Independence. Consider this penultimate line from the second paragraph:

The history of the present King of Great Britain is a history of repeated injuries and usurpations, all having in direct object the establishment of an absolute Tyranny over these States.

Here we have the conspiracy theory that I discussed previously, in which blame is placed squarely on the king. Yet just two years earlier, in *A Summary View of the Rights of British America*, Jefferson had attacked Parliament, not the king. Indeed, in *A Summary View*—which was originally intended to be instructions for Virginia delegates to the

Second Continental Congress—Jefferson recommends that "an humble and dutiful address be presented to his Majesty, begging leave to lay before him, as Chief Magistrate of the British empire, the united complaints of his Majesty's subjects in America." The king, Jefferson goes on to say, "is no more than chief officer of the people, appointed by the laws, and circumscribed with definite powers, to assist working the great machine of government."

As Jefferson saw the matter, the king should function as an impartial arbiter who resolves disputes among otherwise autonomous legislatures within the British Empire. Americans owed allegiance only to the king, so he had the reciprocal duty to intervene when Parliament usurped power that properly belonged to the Americans and their own legislative bodies.

Over the next two years, as Jefferson and other Americans became convinced that the king had not only defaulted on this duty but was also the primary culprit in the conspiracy to strip Americans of their rights and freedoms, they realized that they had no impartial arbiter to whom they could appeal for the redress of grievances. Americans were thereby thrown into a textbook case of the state of nature, a social condition with no impartial arbiter to resolve disputes. Independence was simply a logical corollary of this situation.

This is why the Declaration focuses on the king rather than on Parliament. In an allusion to the theory of de facto independence, it claims that the king "has abdicated Government here, by declaring us out of his Protection, and waging War against us." Thus, with the king having violated his part of the social contract, it became "necessary" for Americans to declare that they no longer acknowledged any allegiance to Great Britain. They were free "to assume among the Powers of the earth, the separate and equal station to which the Laws of Nature and of Nature's God entitle them."

We can now appreciate why many American revolutionaries detested being called "rebels." They were *not* rebels and they were *not* engaged in a rebellion, as their critics and enemies claimed.

In 1774, an American defender of the British wrote: "It is a universal truth that he who would excite a rebellion, is at heart as great a tyrant as ever wielded the iron rod of oppression." An irate John Adams shot back:

> We are not exciting a rebellion. Opposition, nay, open avowed resistance by arms, against usurpation and lawless violence, is not rebellion by the law of God or the land. Do not beg the question . . . and then give yourself airs of triumph. Remember . . . that the word rebel is a convertible term.

John Adams may have been an eccentric man, but this was not an eccentric argument. On the contrary, Adams was invoking a standard Radical Whig doctrine with a long history. John Locke put it this way in his *Second Treatise of Government*:

> Rebellion being an Opposition, not to Persons, but Authority, which is founded only in the Constitutions and Laws of the Government; those, whoever they be, who by force break through, and by force justifie their violation of them, are truly and properly *Rebels*. For when men, by entering into Society and Civil Government, have excluded force, and introduced Laws for the preservation of Property, Peace, and Unity amongst themselves; those who set up force again in opposition to the Laws, do *Rebellare*, that is, bring back again the state of War, and are properly Rebels.

According to Locke and other Radical Whigs, a state of war exists whenever a person repeatedly uses force without legitimate authority. If a king exceeds his legitimate authority, he reverts to the status of a private renegade—a "rebel" against the constitution and natural justice—so his former subjects may use force against him, as they would against any outlaw, in self-defense. This was exactly how revolutionary Americans viewed the conflict with Britain. The king and his political minions were the *true* rebels, not those Americans who wished only to defend their rights and freedoms.

PART 2

The Declaration of Independence

7

"That Audacious Document": Notes on the Declaration of Independence

When modern readers think of the Declaration of Independence, they usually associate it with the celebrated second paragraph. This paragraph begins:

> We hold these truths to be self-evident, that all men are created equal, that they are endowed by their Creator with certain unalienable Rights, that among these are Life, Liberty and the pursuit of Happiness.—That to

secure these rights, Governments are instituted among Men, deriving their just powers from the consent of the governed,—That whenever any Form of Government becomes destructive of these ends, it is the Right of the People to alter or to abolish it, and to institute new Government, laying its foundation on such principles and organizing its powers in such form, as to them shall seem most likely to effect their Safety and Happiness.

Later in the Declaration, we find the list of grievances—those "Facts . . . submitted to a candid world" that explain *why* Americans were justified in dissolving "the political bands" that connected them to Britain, and why they had a right "to assume among the Powers of the earth, the separate and equal station to which the Laws of Nature and of Nature's God entitle them."

Few Americans today are familiar with the Declaration's grievances, but to most readers in 1776 they were far more important than the political principles summarized in the second paragraph. Consider a critique of the Declaration written in 1776 by the English barrister John Lind. Titled *An Answer to the Declaration of the American Congress*, this 132-page book bypasses the second paragraph and focuses instead on the grievances listed in "that audacious document."

We find the same focus in another critique of the Declaration, also published in 1776, by the American loyalist and former governor of Massachusetts, Thomas Hutchinson. In *Strictures Upon the Declaration of the Congress at Philadelphia*, Hutchinson declares that the British Parliament must be the "sole judge" of the actions of the American Congress, so it would be "impertinent" for him "to show in what case a *whole people* may be justified in rising up in oppugnation [i.e., opposition] to the powers of a government, altering or abolishing them, and substituting, in whole or in part, new powers in their stead; or in what sense all men are created equal; or how far life, liberty, and the pursuit of happiness may be said to be unalienable."

Nevertheless, while declining to discuss the political philosophy summarized in the Declaration, Hutchinson could not resist taking this passing swipe: "I could wish to ask the Delegates of Maryland, Virginia, and the Carolinas, how their constituents justify the depriving more than an hundred thousand Africans of their rights to liberty, and *the pursuit of happiness*, and in some degree to their lives, if these rights are so absolutely unalienable." Hutchinson goes on to state his intention "to show the false representation made of the facts which are alleged to be evidence of injuries and usurpations, and the special motives to Rebellion."

The significance of the list of grievances is poignantly illustrated by the dilemma of Peter Van Schaack, a New Yorker who suffered a crisis of conscience in his effort to determine which side he should take in the conflict between America and Britain.

Van Schaack was no Tory. On the contrary, he repudiated the doctrine of passive obedience and supported American resistance to what he regarded as oppressive measures by the British government. But Van Schaack understood that a wide chasm separates *resistance* to particular unjust laws from *revolution* against an established government. This passage from the Declaration expresses the principle involved:

> Prudence, indeed, will dictate that governments long established should not be changed for light and transient causes; and accordingly all experience hath shown that mankind are more disposed to suffer, while evils are sufferable, than to right themselves by abolishing the forms to which they are accustomed. But when a long train of abuses and usurpations, pursuing invariably the same object evinces a design to reduce them under absolute despotism, it is their right, it is their duty, to throw off such government, and to provide new guards for their future security.

This was a key part of the Whig theory of revolution: Before revolution can be justified, it must be shown that the injustices of a government are not merely isolated and unrelated events but are part of an overall *plan* to establish despotism.

Here was the sticking point for Van Schaack and many other Americans who agreed with the political philosophy of the Declaration. Even if some measures of the British government were oppressive, were those measures part of a deliberate *design* to establish "absolute despotism" in America? If this question could not be answered in the affirmative, then a revolution could *not* be justified—and this is why the list of grievances was viewed as the most crucial feature of the Declaration.

After secluding himself at his New York farm to reread and study the works of important political philosophers—including Locke, Vattel, Grotius, and Pufendorf—Van Schaack reached the following conclusion:

> My difficulty arises from this, that taking the whole of the acts [of the British government] complained of together, they do not, I think, manifest a system of slavery, but may fairly be imputed to human frailty, and the difficulty of the subject. Most of them seem to have sprung out of particular occasions, and are

unconnected with each other, and some of them are precisely of the nature of other acts made before the commencement of his present Majesty's reign, which is the era when the supposed design of subjugating the colonies began.... In short, I think those acts may have been passed without a preconcerted plan of enslaving us, and it appears to me that the more favorable construction ought ever to be put on the conduct of our rulers. I cannot therefore think the government dissolved.... I cannot see any principle of regard for my country, which will authorize me in taking up arms.

Van Schaack—a close friend of John Jay (a coauthor of *The Federalist Papers* and first chief justice of the U.S. Supreme Court)—sympathized with the American cause, so he refused to fight as a loyalist. He moved to England and remained there for seven years, after which he returned to New York and resumed his law practice.

It is interesting to compare Van Schaack's analysis of the Declaration with the assessments of the two critics mentioned previously. Whereas Van Schaack did not challenge the accuracy of specific grievances, claiming instead that they did not establish a conspiracy, Lind and Hutchinson analyzed each allegation, point by point, and rejected *each* as unjustified.

Indeed, Hutchinson claimed that American radicals had desired independence for many years and that the list of grievances was concocted to serve as a rationale for a decision that had already been made.

The preceding examples illustrate why the list of grievances was widely regarded as the crux of the Declaration. Many critics of independence, including some American loyalists, agreed with the political principles articulated in the second paragraph. Their problem was the same as the one that haunted Van Schaack; namely: Did the actions of the British government, however unwise or unjust they may have been, signify a deliberate design to extinguish American freedom?

When opponents of the Declaration criticized its political principles, as expressed in the second paragraph, they typically resorted to ridicule rather than undertake a serious analysis. A case in point is found in the *Scots Magazine,* a periodical (edited by James Boswell and published in Edinburgh) that closely followed events in America. When the Declaration was printed in the August 1776 issue of this periodical, a sarcastic note was added that criticized its statement of unalienable rights. This note reads, in part:

> The meaning of these words the Congress appear not
> at all to understand, among which are life, liberty,

and the pursuit of happiness. Let us put some of these words together.—All men are endowed by their Creator with the unalienable right of life. How far they may be endowed with this unalienable right I do not say, but, sure I am, these gentry assume to themselves an unalienable right of talking nonsense. Was it ever heard since the introduction of blunders into the world, that life was a man's right? Life or animation is of the essence of human nature, and is that without which one is not a man; and therefore to call life a right, is to betray a total ignorance of the meaning of words. A living man, i.e., a man with life, hath a right to a great many things; but to say that a man with life hath a right to be a man with life, is so purely American, that I believe the texture of no other brain upon the face of the earth will admit the idea. Whatever it may be, I have tried to make an idea out of it, but own I am unable. . . . The word unalienable signifies that which is not alienable, and that which is not alienable is what can not be transferred so as to become another's; so their unalienable right is a right which they cannot transfer to a broomstick or a cabbage-stalk; and because they cannot transfer their own lives from themselves to a cabbage-stalk, therefore they think it absolutely necessary that they should rebel; and, out of a decent respect to the opinions of mankind, allege this as one of the causes which impels them to separate themselves from those to whom they owe obedience.

After this bit of sophistry, the critic makes a more credible point:

The next assigned cause and ground of their rebellion is, that every man hath an unalienable right to liberty; and here the words, as it happens, are not nonsense; but then they are not true; slaves there are in America; and where there are slaves, their liberty is alienated. If the Creator hath endowed man with an unalienable right to liberty, no reason in the world will justify the abridgement of that liberty, and a man hath a right to do everything that he thinks proper without control or restraint; and upon the same principle, there can be no such things as servants, subjects, or government of any kind whatsoever. In a word, every law that hath been in the world since the formation of Adam, gives the lie to this self-evident truth (as they are pleased to term it); because every law, divine or human, that is or hath been in the world, is an abridgement of man's liberty. Their next self-evident truth and ground of rebellion is, that they have an unalienable right to the pursuit of happiness.

So what did Thomas Jefferson have in mind when he wrote about the unalienable rights to life, liberty, and the pursuit of happiness? I will discuss this issue in Chapter 8.

8

Was Thomas Jefferson a Plagiarist?

Probably no sentence—or, in this case, fragment of a sentence—in the history of political thought has received more attention from historians and elicited more controversy than this passage from the Declaration of Independence:

> We hold these truths to be self-evident, that all men are created equal, that they are endowed by their Creator with certain unalienable Rights, that among these are Life, Liberty and the pursuit of Happiness.

Here is how this passage was originally written, in what Thomas Jefferson called his "original Rough draught" of the Declaration:

> We hold these truths to be sacred & undeniable; that all men are created equal & independant, that from that equal creation they derive rights inherent & inalienable, among which are the preservation of life, & liberty, & the pursuit of happiness.

On June 12, 1776, within a day of the time that Jefferson probably began writing the Declaration, George Mason's draft of the Virginia Declaration of Rights was published in the *Pennsylvania Gazette*. This document reads, in part:

> That all men are born equally free and independant, and have certain inherent natural rights, of which they cannot, by any compact, deprive or divest their posterity, among which are the enjoyment of life and liberty, with the means of acquiring and possessing property, and pursuing and obtaining happiness and safety.

The similarities between Mason's document and Jefferson's rough draft have led many historians to conclude that Jefferson drew from Mason while writing the Declaration. Jefferson's biographer Dumas Malone (*Jefferson the Virginian*) speculates that there may have been a "direct influence," while Pauline Maier (*American Scripture: Making the Declaration of Independence*) goes so far as to say that Jefferson had Mason's draft "in hand" while working on the Declaration of Independence.

Such efforts to trace to earlier sources both the ideas expressed in Jefferson's Declaration and the particular wording he used are nothing new. Jefferson's contemporaries engaged in the same exercise, sometimes going so far as to accuse him of plagiarism, in effect. For example, Richard Henry Lee, Jefferson's fellow Virginian who made the original resolution for American independence, claimed that Jefferson had copied from John Locke's *Second Treatise of Government*.

On April 30, 1819, the *Raleigh Register and North Carolina Gazette* published a document that has become known as the Mecklenburg Declaration of Independence. This newspaper article begins:

> It is probably not known to many of our readers, that the citizens of Mecklenburg county, in this state [North Carolina], made a declaration of independence a year before Congress made theirs.

The Mecklenburg Declaration of Independence, which was supposedly issued by a convention held in Charlotte on

May 20, 1775, contains phrases that are identical to those that Jefferson used over a year later. Shortly after John Adams read a reprint of the Mecklenburg Declaration in the *Essex Register* (June 5, 1819), he wrote to a friend:

> A few weeks ago I received an Essex Register, containing resolutions of independence by a county in North Carolina. . . . I was struck with so much astonishment on reading this document, that I could not help inclosing it immediately to Mr. Jefferson, who must have seen it, in the time of it, for he has copied the spirit, the sense, and the expression of it verbatim, into his Declaration.

After Jefferson read the Mecklenburg Declaration, he wrote to Adams, "I believe it spurious." Although Adams claimed to be "entirely convinced" by Jefferson's reasons—some of which were sound and some of which were not—his longstanding jealousy of the credit that Jefferson had received for the Declaration of Independence led him to write to another correspondent:

> I could as soon believe that the dozen flowers of the Hydrangia now before my Eyes were the work of chance, as that the Mecklenburg Resolutions and Mr. Jefferson's declaration were not derived the one from the other.

Although Jefferson was correct—the Mecklenburg Declaration is indeed spurious—the controversy raged throughout the 19th century and into the early 20th century. In the *New York Review* of March 1837, a defender of the Mecklenburg Declaration, one Dr. Hawks, expressly accused Jefferson of plagiarism—and this charge has been repeated, if only implicitly, by other defenders of the "Mec Dec," especially North Carolinians.

In "Why North Carolinians Believe in the Mecklenburg Declaration of Independence," the transcript of a speech delivered to the Mecklenburg Historical Society on October 11, 1894, Dr. George W. Graham stated:

> There is no event of the American Revolution about which more has been written than the Mecklenburg Declaration of Independence of May 20th, 1775, and at the present time upwards of four score articles are in print concerning it. Some were prepared because the writers desired to see an account of this bold action recorded in the history of North Carolina; some because it was feared that, if the authenticity of this declaration was established, Thomas Jefferson would be proclaimed a plagiarist.

The most thorough analysis of the Mecklenburg Declaration was published in 1907 by William Henry Hoyt: *The Mecklenburg Declaration of Independence: A Study of Evidence Showing That the Alleged Early Declaration of Independence by Mecklenburg County, North Carolina, on May 20, 1775, Is Spurious.* It is virtually impossible for any objective person to read this exhaustive refutation of the Mec Dec Myth and still believe that Thomas Jefferson was a plagiarist.

Lost causes die hard, as we see on the website for the Mecklenburg Historical Association (September 2011), which advertises a lecture by Judge Chase B. Saunders, a fifth-generation North Carolinian. His presentation, "A Defense of the Mecklenburg Declaration of Independence," is summarized as follows:

A motion for appropriate relief seeking the reexamination of the record of history by the academic community and exoneration of the drafters of the Mecklenburg Declaration of Independence.[2]

A motion seeking the trial of UNC Professor Charles Phillips for academic misconduct in his 1853 publication, defaming the drafters and declaring the episode a fraud, for wanton negligence in conducting his research and thereby failing to meet generally accepted standards of academic research and materially deviated from said standards.

What exactly was the academic crime of Professor Charles Phillips? Well, Phillips, having examined the original documents associated with the Mecklenburg Declaration, detected fraud and forgery, and he said so in an article published in the *North Carolina University Magazine* (May 1853). As Phillips explained in 1858, "All the story about the 20th of May could not stand before cool and fair criticism. . . . To me, the assertion, or insinuation, that Jefferson ever borrowed from Mecklenburg is just ridiculous."

(Whether overt fraud was involved in this complex story is problematic. For a useful summary of the explanation accepted by most historians today, see Pauline Maier, *American Scripture: Making the Declaration of Independence*.)[3]

In 1823, four years after the publication of the Mecklenburg Declaration, another controversy erupted—one that was precipitated by the embittered Federalist Timothy Pickering, a political enemy of Jefferson who had served as secretary of state during the administration of John Adams. This controversy focused not on the wording of the Declaration of Independence but on the originality of the ideas expressed therein.

In his Fourth of July oration, Pickering argued that Jefferson had received too much credit for the Declaration, that many other Americans had expressed the same ideas before Jefferson wrote the document. There was nothing surprising in this effort to undermine Jefferson's contribution, considering that it came from an ardent Federalist and old political enemy. More surprising was this passage that Pickering read from a letter he had received the previous year from John Adams:

> As you justly observe, there is not an idea in it but what had been hackneyed in Congress for two years before. The substance of it is contained the declaration of rights and the violation of those rights in the Journals of Congress in 1774. Indeed, the essence of it is contained in a pamphlet, voted and printed by the town of Boston, before the first Congress met, composed by James Otis, as I suppose, in one of his lucid intervals, and pruned and polished by Samuel Adams.

Jefferson responded with remarkable grace to this slight by Adams, especially considering that the two men had resumed their old friendship a decade earlier, after years of political animosity. In an oft-quoted letter to James Madison (August 30, 1823), Jefferson wrote:

> Pickering's observations, and Mr. Adams' in addition, "that [the Declaration] contained no new ideas, that it is a commonplace compilation, its sentiments hacknied in Congress for two years before, and its essence contained in Otis' pamphlet," may all be true. Of that I am not to be the judge. . . . Otis' pamphlet I never saw, and whether I had gathered my ideas from reading or reflection I do not know. I know only that I turned to neither book nor pamphlet while writing it. I did not consider it as any part of my charge to invent new ideas altogether, and to offer no sentiment which had ever been expressed before.

As Jefferson explained to a correspondent in 1825, just 14 months before his death:

> Neither aiming at originality of principle or sentiment, nor yet copied from any particular and previous writing, it was intended to be an expression of the American mind, and to give to that expression the proper tone and spirit called for by the occasion. All its authority rests then on the harmonizing sentiments

of the day, whether expressed in conversation, letters, printed essays, or in the elementary books of public right, as Aristotle, Cicero, Locke, Sidney, etc.

After decades of studying the Declaration and the standard sources of Real (or Radical) Whig ideas, I have found no compelling reasons to doubt Jefferson's claim that he "turned to neither book nor pamphlet while writing" the Declaration, and that it was not "copied from any particular and previous writing." My reasons will be presented in the next chapter, but before concluding this chapter, I wish to comment briefly on another theory of the Declaration that qualifies as a cult favorite.

In 1966, during my third year of high school, I read a book titled *Thomas Paine, Author of the Declaration of Independence.*[4] The author, American freethinker Joseph Lewis, presented what appeared to be an impressive array of facts and arguments to support the thesis that Thomas Paine, not Thomas Jefferson, was the real author of the Declaration (or at least most of it).

Puzzled by what I had read, I took the book to school, showed it to my American history teacher, and solicited his opinion. He showed considerable interest and asked to borrow the book.

I never saw the book again. According to my teacher, it mysteriously disappeared from the teachers' lounge after he left it there overnight. I got five dollars for my loss, which was twice what I had originally paid, but I never quite believed his story. I suspected my teacher overpaid me out of guilt because he wanted to keep the book for himself.

By the time I read Lewis's book, I had been reading books by and about Thomas Paine for nearly two years. I knew that Paine had been denigrated because of his authorship of *Age of Reason*—Theodore Roosevelt, for example, called Paine "that filthy little atheist," even though Paine, a deist, attacked atheism in *Age of Reason*—and I shared the desire of many freethinkers to see Paine restored to his rightful place in American history.

But Lewis's thesis, if true, would mean that Thomas Jefferson, who explicitly claimed authorship and who, in his own epitaph, listed the Declaration as one of the three achievements for which he wished to be remembered, was one of the biggest liars in American history. It would also mean that Thomas Paine, who never so much as hinted at any connection with the Declaration, was one of the most modest figures in American history. It is difficult to say which assumption is more unbelievable.

Some years later, I obtained another copy of *Thomas Paine, Author of the Declaration of Independence* and read it again. By that time, I knew quite a bit about Thomas Jefferson and the Declaration, so what had previously seemed like a plausible case then struck me as a string of incorrect assertions and unsubstantiated speculations.

I subsequently learned that most of the arguments by Lewis had been circulating for at least a century before his book was published in 1947. The claim that Paine wrote the Declaration goes back at least to the mid-19th century; the standard arguments were repeated time and again in books published by Peter Eckler, the Truth Seeker, and other freethought publishers. It was even given some credibility, if in a scaled-down version, by Moncure Conway in his excellent two-volume *Life of Thomas Paine* (1892).

My early exposure to the Thomas Paine thesis taught me a valuable lesson—namely, that historical quackery is more common than one might think and that books on history should always be read with a critical eye.

9

The Philosophy of the Declaration of Independence

On June 7, 1776, the Virginian Richard Henry Lee introduced the following resolution on the floor of the Second Continental Congress:

> That these United Colonies are, and of right ought to be, free and independent States, that they are absolved from all allegiance to the British Crown, and that all political connection between them and the State of Great Britain is, and ought to be, totally dissolved.

After considering this resolution twice (June 8 and 10), Congress postponed further consideration until July 1. Although the resolution was certain to pass, unanimous ratification by the colonies was wanted, and for various reasons this was not possible until some glitches had been worked out.

Lee's resolution for American independence passed on July 2 (not July 4). This prompted an excited John Adams to write to his wife, Abigail:

> The Second Day of July 1776, will be the most memorable Epocha, in the History of America. I am apt to believe that it will be celebrated, by succeeding Generations, as the great anniversary Festival. It ought to be commemorated, as the Day of Deliverance by solemn Acts of Devotion to God Almighty. It ought to be solemnized with Pomp and Parade, with Shews, Games, Sports, Guns, Bells, Bonfires and Illuminations from one End of this Continent to the other from this Time forward forever more.

On June 11, Congress appointed a Committee of Five to draft a declaration: Thomas Jefferson, John Adams, Benjamin Franklin, Roger Sherman, and Robert R. Livingston.

Events become somewhat murky after this point because Jefferson and Adams provided different accounts in later years. An 88-year-old Adams claimed that he and Jefferson were appointed as a subcommittee to prepare a draft, after which Adams persuaded Jefferson to write the document.

An 80-year-old Jefferson disputed this account. He denied that a subcommittee had ever been formed, claiming instead that the entire committee "unanimously pressed on myself alone to undertake the draught."

A more serious discrepancy between the accounts of Adams and Jefferson pertains to how the Declaration was actually drafted. In his *Autobiography* (1805), Adams recalled that the Committee of Five held several meetings, during which an outline of the Declaration was drawn up to serve as a guide for the draftsman.

Jefferson gave no indication of such an outline, suggesting instead that he had written the Declaration from scratch. It was only after he had completed the "original Rough draught" that Jefferson submitted the document to Adams and Franklin separately, soliciting changes that he later described as "two or three short and verbal alterations." But, Jefferson continued, "even this is laying more stress on mere composition than it merits, for that alone was mine."

The rough draft to which Jefferson refers is one of the most fascinating documents in American history. In 1945, Jefferson scholar Julian P. Boyd said of it:

> There can scarcely be any question but that the Rough Draft is the most extraordinarily interesting document in American history. . . . For it embodies in its text and in its multiplicity of corrections, additions, and deletions all, or almost all, of the Declaration as it was at every stage of its journey from its origin in the parlor of Graff's home to its emergence in full glory as the authenticated and official charter of liberty of the American people.[5]

For those who wish to understand the political philosophy of the Declaration, the significant part is the famous second paragraph. The first part of the second paragraph, as painstakingly reconstructed by Carl Becker in 1922 (*The Declaration of Independence: A Study in the History of Political Ideas*), originally read:

> We hold these truths to be sacred & undeniable; that all men are created equal & independant, that from that equal creation they derive rights inherent & inalienable, among which are the preservation of

life, & liberty, & the pursuit of happiness; that to secure these ends, governments are instituted among men, deriving their just powers from the consent of the governed; that whenever any form of government shall become destructive of these ends, it is the right of the people to alter or to abolish it, & to institute new government, laying it's foundation on such principles & organizing it's powers in such form, as to them shall seem most likely to effect their safety and happiness.

We have here a brilliantly concise statement of what historians call "Real" (or "Radical") Whig ideology, a libertarian political philosophy commonly associated with John Locke. But before I delve into this philosophy I want to comment on a point of historical trivia.

The Declaration we know today refers to *unalienable* rights, but Jefferson used the word *inalienable*. Jefferson did not make this change, nor does the change appear to have been made by Congress while it was considering the draft submitted by the Committee of Five. So who made this change, and why? We don't know. *Unalienable* first appears in John Dunlap's initial printing of the Declaration (July 5), which was inserted in the rough *Journals of the Continental Congress*. It also appears in the corrected *Journals* and in the engrossed parchment version, which was signed by delegates on August 2. (Contrary to the later recollections of Jefferson and Adams, no signing occurred on July 4.)

Becker suggested that John Adams might have been responsible for the change: "Adams was one of the committee which supervised the printing of the text adopted by Congress, and it may have been at his suggestion that the change was made in printing." Boyd (editor of the massive Princeton edition of *The Papers of Thomas Jefferson*) proposed a different theory: "This alteration may possibly have been made by the printer [John Dunlap] rather than at the suggestion of Congress."

Fortunately for my purpose here, this minor mystery is of no consequence. Both *inalienable* and *unalienable* were used throughout the 18th century; they were merely variant spellings of the same word. (*Unalienable* appears to have been more common.) Far more significant is why Jefferson felt the need to specify inalienable rights at all, rather than referring simply to natural rights, inherent rights, and so forth.

Inalienable (or unalienable) rights were regarded as fundamental corollaries of man's nature, especially his reason and volition, so these rights could never be surrendered or transferred to another person (including a government), even with the agent's consent. A man can no more transfer his inalienable rights than he can transfer his moral agency, his ability to reason, and so forth. This means that inalienable rights could never have been transferred to government in a social contract, so no government can properly claim jurisdiction over them.

This argument from inalienable rights was important because of an ambiguity in traditional social contract theory. The social contract was more of a theoretical construct than a historical reality, so disagreements inevitably raged over which rights had been delegated to government and which rights had not. After all, no legitimate complaint can be made about the violation of a right if a government has gained proper jurisdiction over that right in the social contract. Government, for instance, cannot function without money, so the transfer of a minimal amount of property to government, collected in the form of taxes, was commonly seen as the prime example of a right that has been alienated in a social contract.

According to this approach, legitimate disagreements may occur between subjects and rulers when alienable rights are involved, but no such disputes are justified over the question of inalienable rights. Government cannot claim any jurisdiction over such rights, because inalienable rights, by their very nature, could never have been transferred to government in the first place. Therefore, there can be no excuse for the violation of inalienable rights. This is the crucial bright-line test that enables us to distinguish the incidental or well-intentioned violation of rights, which even just governments may occasionally commit, from the deliberate and inexcusable violations of a tyrannical government.

We thus see why Jefferson focused on inalienable rights in his effort to fasten the charge of tyranny on the British government. The violation of inalienable rights was a defining characteristic of a tyrannical government, and only against such a government is revolution justified.

Although this basic argument can be found in John Locke's *Second Treatise of Government*, Locke never actually used the word *inalienable* (or *unalienable*) in regard to rights. We do find this terminology, however, in an early book by the Scottish (and Lockean) philosopher Francis Hutcheson.

In *An Inquiry into the Original of Our Ideas of Beauty and Virtue* (1725), Hutcheson discusses an "important Difference of Rights, according as they are Alienable or Unalienable." In order for a right to be alienable, it must "be possible for us in Fact to transfer our Right." Some rights, such as "the Right of private judgment," cannot be transferred because they flow directly from our nature as moral agents, and we cannot transfer our faculties of volition and judgment to other people, as we might transfer a piece of external property.

In "the same way," Hutcheson continues, "a direct Right over our Lives or Limbs, is not alienable to any Person; so that he might at Pleasure put us to death, or maim us."

Hutcheson clearly states the political implications when inalienable rights are violated by government:

> All human Power, or Authority, must consist of a Right transferr'd to any Person or Council, to dispose of the alienable rights of others; and that consequently, there can be no Government so absolute, as to have even an external Right to do or command everything. For wherever any Invasion is made upon unalienable Rights, there must arise either a perfect, or external Right of Resistance. . . . Unalienable Rights are essential Limitations in all Governments.

As indicated by Hutcheson's mention of "perfect" and "external" rights, the doctrine of inalienable rights presupposed a rather elaborate theory of natural rights. Space does not permit a discussion of that theory here. Suffice it to say that the distinction between alienable and inalienable rights had become commonplace by the time Jefferson wrote the Declaration in 1776. It is found in the standard works on natural law familiar to 18th-century Americans, such as that written by Jean-Jacques Burlamaqui, *The Principles of Natural and Politic Law* (1747, 1751).

Among American writers, the distinction between alienable and inalienable rights was frequently invoked by defenders of religious freedom. Perhaps the best example of this was published in 1744 by the dissenting minister Elisha Williams: *The Essential Rights and Liberties of Protestants: A seasonable Plea for The Liberty of Conscience, and The Right of private Judgment, in Matters of Religion, Without any Controul from human Authority.*

After designating freedom of conscience as an "unalienable right," Williams explains:

> This I say, I take to be an original right of the humane nature, and so far from being given up by the individuals of a community [in a social contract] that it cannot be given up by them if they should be so weak as to offer it. . . . Whence it follows, the rights of conscience are sacred and equal in all, and strictly speaking unalienable. . . . A man may alienate some branches of his property and give up his right in them to others; but he cannot transfer the rights of conscience, unless he could destroy his rational and moral powers, or substitute some other to be judged for him at the tribunal of God.

Although the appeal to inalienable rights first arose in the context of religious freedom, it was quickly extended to spheres other than religion, as we find in Jefferson's appeal to the inalienable rights of "Life, Liberty and the pursuit of Happiness." This was one of the most significant developments in the history of libertarian thought.

Among the controversies generated by the Declaration's second paragraph, two stand out as especially contentious: (1) Thomas Jefferson's use of *self-evident* to characterize "these truths" expressed in the second paragraph, and (2) the omission of the right to property in the list of inalienable (or unalienable) rights. I shall discuss these problems here.

First, let's consider Jefferson's use of *self-evident*. It would surprise some people to learn how much scholarly attention has been devoted to analyzing what Jefferson meant by *this term*. Morton White (*The Philosophy of the American Revolution*) devotes nearly 90 pages to show that "in the Declaration the use of the word 'self-evident' was directly or indirectly influenced"[6] by John Locke's *Essay Concerning Human Understanding.* Garry Wills (*Inventing America: Jefferson's Declaration of Independence*, 1978)[7] links the meaning of *self-evident* to the Common Sense philosophy of the Scottish philosopher Thomas Reid. W. S. Howell, in a 1961 issue of the *William and Mary Quarterly*, suggests that Jefferson was influenced by a now-obscure logic text (William Duncan's *Elements of Logick*) that he read during his college days at William and Mary.

In my judgment, the most plausible explanation is the one given by Michael P. Zuckert in his excellent book, *The Natural Rights Republic: Studies in the Foundation of the American Political Tradition*.[8] Zuckert maintains that *self-evident* should be understood in a "practical" sense, not as an epistemological theory.

This ongoing hermeneutical exercise is complicated by the fact that *self-evident* was a later revision of Jefferson's rough draft, which originally read "We hold these truths to be sacred & undeniable. . . ." So who crossed out *sacred & undeniable* and wrote *self-evident* above it? And why was this revision made?

Some historians believe *self-evident* is in the handwriting of Benjamin Franklin. The Jeffersonian scholar Julian P. Boyd disagreed, maintaining that the alteration bears the distinctive characteristics of Jefferson's handwriting. But Boyd goes on to argue that John Adams probably suggested the revision.

Fortunately, none of this matters for my purpose here, since Jefferson obviously agreed with the change, regardless of whose idea it was. As Jefferson put it many years later, the revisions made by Franklin and Adams were "merely verbal" and did not affect the meaning of the text.

Jefferson knew that the Declaration would be read aloud to throngs of people throughout the colonies, so he was writing as much for the ear as for the eye. At this stage of composition, before substantial changes were made by Congress, we may safely assume that revisions were made primarily for stylistic reasons. For example, a phrase in the rough draft, "rights inherent & inalienable, among which are the preservation of life, & liberty, & the pursuit of happiness," became "certain unalienable Rights, that among these are Life, Liberty and the pursuit of Happiness"—a definite stylistic improvement without any change of meaning.

We now return to the original question that has generated a cottage industry for historians and philosophers: What did Jefferson mean by *self-evident*?

One good thing about writing overviews of complex subjects is that I can plead space limitations to avoid getting bogged down in technicalities.

In accord with the treatment of Michael Zuckert, I believe it highly unlikely that Jefferson used *self-evident* with any technical epistemological meaning in mind. The epistemological interpretation might be credible if Jefferson had confined his self-evident truths to the inalienable rights of "Life, Liberty and the pursuit of Happiness," but he doesn't stop there. He extends the list to include the purpose for which "Governments are instituted among Men," the doctrine that governments derive their "just powers from the consent of the governed," and "the Right of the People to alter or to abolish" an unjust government. It exceeds the limits of credibility to contend that Jefferson viewed *all* "these truths" as epistemologically self-evident, as if they should be accepted without argument or demonstration.

Note that Jefferson does not say that "these truths" *are* self-evident. Rather, he says, "*We hold* these truths to be self-evident. . . ." Jefferson is articulating what Francis Bacon once called "middle axioms"—namely, propositions that, though not self-evident in themselves, are accepted as axiomatic for the purpose of a particular argument. In later life, Jefferson characterized the Declaration's political principles as "an expression of the American mind." It was not his intention to invent new principles but merely to summarize the principles that were widely accepted in America and that constituted the *theoretical foundation* of American independence.

Jefferson does not argue for the principles expressed in the second paragraph, much less attempt to prove them. He presents them as a given—as *contextually* axiomatic, so to speak. We can better appreciate the reason for this approach by taking a look at the opening paragraph of the Declaration:

> When in the Course of human events, it becomes necessary for one people to dissolve the political

bands which have connected them with another, and to assume among the Powers of the earth, the separate and equal station to which the Laws of Nature and of Nature's God entitle them, a decent respect to the opinions of mankind requires that they should declare the causes which impel them to the separation.

It should be kept in mind that the Declaration did not actually declare the independence of the American colonies from Great Britain; this occurred on July 2, 1776, two days before the Declaration was approved by the Second Continental Congress on July 4. It fell to Jefferson, as part of a five-man committee, to explain and justify this momentous decision.

Jefferson's use of the word *impel* is significant, as is his use of *necessary*. Jefferson didn't feel the need to justify the Lockean principles expressed in the second paragraph, since he believed they were *already* accepted by most Americans. But, as I explained earlier in this book, many of these Americans either were undecided about independence or opposed it outright. The Declaration was addressed as much to these people as it was to "mankind" at large. Jefferson wished to convince fence-sitters and skeptics that independence was not a reckless scheme hatched by hotheaded, seditious radicals who were eager to grab power for themselves. (This was the standard line of hawks within the British government.) Rather, independence was rendered *necessary* by the despotic measures of the British government. Hence the crucial significance of the list of grievances, to which the second paragraph served as a theoretical prelude.

Thus, as Zuckert points out, Jefferson intended "self-evident" to be understood in a *practical* sense, not as the application of an epistemological theory of self-evident knowledge. There was no way, within the span of a brief document, that Jefferson could have demonstrated the principles articulated in the second paragraph, nor was there any need to do this. Jefferson said "We hold these truths to be self-evident" because he wished to express their axiomatic status among the advocates of American Independence. The purpose of the Declaration was *not* to *justify* these fundamental principles but to *apply* them to the crises with Britain, and this application is found in the list of grievances.

Strictly considered, "self-evident" was not the best choice of words; Jefferson's original formulation ("sacred & undeniable") was more precise. But those philosophers who wring their hands over this bit of literary license should keep in mind that Jefferson's contemporaries, many of whom were well-schooled in philosophy, appeared to have had no problem with "self-evident." They knew exactly what Jefferson meant.

Now let's consider the omission of the right to property in the list of inalienable (or unalienable) rights. After stating that men "are endowed by their Creator with certain unalienable Rights," the Declaration goes on to say that "among these are Life, Liberty and the pursuit of Happiness."

The controversy over this clause, which has been considerable, is owing not to what it says but to what it fails to say. Why did Jefferson omit property from his trinity of inalienable rights? Could it be, as some leftist historians have argued, that Jefferson was a quasi-socialist who did not hold property rights in the same esteem as his contemporaries did? Even one of Jefferson's best biographers, Willard Sterne Randall, contends that Jefferson's "choice of words 'pursuit of happiness' over John Locke's 'property' marked a sharp break with the Whig doctrine of English middle-class property rights."

With due respect to Randall and similar commentators, such interpretations have no justification whatsoever.

The first thing to note is that Jefferson did mention property, along with life and liberty, in some other writings. For example, he wrote: "The End of Government would be defeated by the British Parliament exercising a Power over the Lives, the Property, and the Liberty of the American Subject; who are not, and, from the local Circumstances, cannot, be there represented," and "To obtain Redress of the Grievances, which threaten Destruction of the Lives, Liberty, and Property, of his Majesty's Subjects. . . ."

The second thing to note is that Jefferson refers specifically to *inalienable* rights, and he states that "*among these*" inalienable rights are the rights to life, liberty, and the pursuit of happiness—thereby indicating that *his list is not exhaustive.*

Why Jefferson did not include property in his partial list of inalienable rights is obviously a matter of conjecture, but the reason should be fairly obvious to historians who understand the ambiguous meaning of *property* in Jefferson's day. It had two distinct meanings. Property was an *inalienable* right according to one meaning, whereas it was an *alienable* right according to another meaning. Given this ambiguity, to refer to property as an inalienable right would have been confusing without further explanation, and Jefferson was not writing a philosophical treatise.

When we speak of property today, we usually mean a thing or an object that is owned, something we have a moral and/or legal right to use and dispose of, such as a pencil. This pencil, we say, is my property; I own it; I have a right to use it, give it away, sell it, or destroy it.

During the 17th and 18th centuries, the word *property* was often used in a broader sense to mean rightful dominion, or moral jurisdiction, over something. As the Lockean William Wollaston put it during the early 18th century: "To have the property of any thing and to have the sole right of using and disposing of it are the same thing: they are equipollent expressions." This broad conception permitted Wollaston to speak of a man's "*property* in his own happiness."

Whereas we would say "This pencil is my property," earlier libertarians were more likely to say "I have a property in this pencil." When John Locke argued that the proper function of government is to protect property, he explained that by *property* he meant a person's "Life, Liberty, and Estate." This usage is what Locke had in mind when he wrote that "every Man has a *Property* in his own *Person.*"

In Jefferson's day both meanings of *property* were common, but the older usage, according to which I would be said to have *a property in* my pencil, was giving way to the modern usage, according to which this pencil would be said to be *my property*. This dual usage was discussed by James Madison in 1792, and his treatment deserves to be quoted at length:

> This term [property] in its particular application means "that dominion which one man claims and exercises over the external things of the world, in exclusion of every other individual."

In its larger and juster meaning, it embraces everything to which a man may attach a value and have a right, and *which leave to every one else the like advantage.*

In the former sense, a man's land, or merchandize, or money is called his property.

In the latter sense, a man has a property in his opinions and the free communication of them.

He has a property of peculiar value in his religious opinions, and in the profession and practice dictated by them.

He has a property very dear to him in the safety and liberty of his person.

He has an equal property in the free use of his faculties and free choice of the objects on which to employ them.

In a word, as a man is said to have a right to his property, he may be equally said to have a property in his rights.

Property in the broad sense—that is, the right to exercise moral jurisdiction over one's person and labor and the fruits of one's labor—was viewed as an inalienable right; to have moral jurisdiction over that which is essential to one's survival is inextricably linked to one's moral agency and so can never be transferred or surrendered. But this is not true of property in the narrower sense of material objects that are owned; one can clearly transfer one's title to pencils and other material goods.

Indeed, the title to a certain amount of property, collected in the form of taxes, was said to have been implicitly surrendered in the Lockean version of the social contract, since revenue was needed for a government to function. It would therefore have been confusing for Jefferson to have included "property" in his partial list of inalienable rights. He would have needed to draw the same distinction that Madison did between two meanings of *property*, and this would have transformed the Declaration from a brief manifesto into a lengthy treatise.

Given many statements by Jefferson, there is no reason to think he would have disagreed with this very Lockean conclusion by Madison:

> Government is instituted to protect property of every sort; as well that which lies in the various rights of individuals, as that which the term particularly expresses. This being the end of government, that alone is a *just* government which *impartially* secures to every man, whatever is his *own*.

Notes

[1] R. R. Palmer, *The Age of the Democratic Revolution* (Princeton, NJ: Princeton University Press, 2014).

[2] Mecklenburg Historical Association, *MHA News* 8, no. 3 (September 2011), http://meckdec.org/images/september2011.pdf.

[3] Pauline Maier, *American Scripture: Making the Declaration of Independence* (New York: Vintage Books, 1977), pp. 172–74.

[4] Joseph Lewis, *Thomas Paine, Author of the Declaration of Independence* (New York: Freethought Press Association, 1947).

[5] Julian P. Boyd, *The Declaration of Independence: The Evolution of the Text* (Washington: Library of Congress, 1999), p. 26.

[6] Morton White, *The Philosophy of the American Revolution* (Oxford, UK: Oxford University Press, 1978).

[7] Garry Wills, *Inventing America: Jefferson's Declaration of Independence* (New York: Doubleday, 1978).

[8] Michael P. Zuckert, *The Natural Rights Republic: Studies in the Foundation of the American Political Tradition* (Notre Dame, IN: University of Notre Dame Press, 1996).

Index

Libertarianism.org

Liberty. It's a simple idea and the linchpin of a complex system of values and practices: justice, prosperity, responsibility, toleration, cooperation, and peace. Many people believe that liberty is the core political value of modern civilization itself, the one that gives substance and form to all the other values of social life. They're called libertarians.

Libertarianism.org is the Cato Institute's treasury of resources about the theory and history of liberty. The book you're holding is a small part of what Libertarianism.org has to offer. In addition to hosting classic texts by historical libertarian figures and original articles from modern-day thinkers, Libertarianism.org publishes podcasts, videos, online introductory courses, and books on a variety of topics within the libertarian tradition.

Cato Institute

Founded in 1977, the Cato Institute is a public policy research foundation dedicated to broadening the parameters of policy debate to allow consideration of more options that are consistent with the principles of limited government, individual liberty, and peace. To that end, the Institute strives to achieve greater involvement of the intelligent, concerned lay public in questions of policy and the proper role of government.

The Institute is named for *Cato's Letters*, libertarian pamphlets that were widely read in the American Colonies in the early 18th century and played a major role in laying the philosophical foundation for the American Revolution.

Despite the achievement of the nation's Founders, today virtually no aspect of life is free from government encroachment. A pervasive intolerance for individual rights is shown by government's arbitrary intrusions into private economic transactions and its disregard for civil liberties. And while freedom around the globe has notably increased in the past several decades, many countries have moved in the opposite direction, and most governments still do not respect or safeguard the wide range of civil and economic liberties.

To address those issues, the Cato Institute undertakes an extensive publications program on the complete spectrum of policy issues. Books, monographs, and shorter studies are commissioned to examine the federal budget, Social Security, regulation, military spending, international trade, and myriad other issues. Major policy conferences are held throughout the year, from which papers are published thrice yearly in the *Cato Journal*. The Institute also publishes the quarterly magazine *Regulation*.

In order to maintain its independence, the Cato Institute accepts no government funding. Contributions are received from foundations, corporations, and individuals, and other revenue is generated from the sale of publications. The Institute is a nonprofit, tax-exempt, educational foundation under Section 501(c)3 of the Internal Revenue Code.

CATO INSTITUTE
1000 Massachusetts Ave., N.W.
Washington, D.C. 20001
www.cato.org

CPSIA information can be obtained
at www.ICGtesting.com
Printed in the USA
LVOW11s2327051117
555042LV00001BA/1/P